Elmira Ontario Book 1 in Colour Photos, Saving Our History One Photo at a Time

Photography
by Barbara Raué
2014

Series Name:
Cruising Ontario

Book 70: Elmira Book 1

Cover photo: 80 Arthur Street South

Series Name: Cruising Ontario
Saving Our History One Photo at a Time

Book 33: Southampton
Book 34: Jarvis
Book 35: Hagersville
Book 36: Caledonia
Book 37: Simcoe
Book 38: Cambridge
Part 1 – Galt Book 1
Book 39: Cambridge
Part 1 – Galt Book 2
Book 40: Cambridge
Part 2 – Preston
Book 41: Cambridge
Part 3 – Hespeler
Book 42: Kitchener 1
Book 43: Kitchener 2
Book 46: Shelburne
Book 47: Alton, Mono
Book 48: London Colour
Book 49: St. Thomas
Book 50: Orangeville 1
Book 51: Orangeville 2
Book 52: Orangeville 3
Book 53: Dundas 1
Book 54: Dundas 2
Book 55: Dundas 3
Book 56: Stratford
Book 57: Hanover
Book 58: NewHamburg1
Book 59: NewHamburg2

Book 60: Waterdown
Book 61: Burlington
Book 62: Stoney Creek
Book 63: Seaforth
Book 64: Aberfoyle,
Morriston and Rockton
Book 65: Eden Mills
Book 66: Ancaster and
Mount Hope
Book 67: Jarvis,Pt.Dover
Book 68: Fergus
Book 69: Elora
Book 70: Elmira Book 1
Book 71: Elmira 2 & Area
Book72:St.Jacobs, St.Clements,
Heidelberg,Crosshill,Bamberg
Book 73: Linwood, Macton

Other Books by Barbara Raue

Coins of Gold

Arrows, Indians and Love

The Life and Times of Barbara
Volume 1: Inventions That Have Enhanced My Life
Volume 2: Entertainment That I Have Enjoyed
Volume 3: East Coast Trips
Volume 4: Olympics Have Always Intrigued Me
Volume 5: Wonders of the World
Volume 6: Caribbean Cruises We Have Enjoyed
Volume 7: Animals
Volume 8: Storms and Other Major Disasters in My Lifetime
Volume 9: Wars, Terrorist Attacks and Major Disasters

The Cromwell Family Book

Laura Secord Discovered

Visit Barbara's website to view all of her books
http://barbararaue.ca

Elmira is the largest community within the Township of Woolwich in the Regional Municipality of Waterloo and is located 15 kilometres (9 miles) to the north of the city of Waterloo.

The land comprising Woolwich Township originally belonged to the Huron and then the Mohawk Indians. The first settlers arrived in Woolwich Township in the late eighteenth century. In 1798, William Wallace, one of the first settlers in the area, was deeded 86,078 acres of land on the Grand River for a cost of $16,364.

In 1806, Wallace sold the major portion of his tract to Mennonites. Benjamin Eby, the secretary of the Germany Company came to the area with his friend Henry Brubacher. The young men liked Wallace's Woolwich. Eby returned to Pennsylvania where he formed a land company. The following year, he returned with a barrel of silver dollars, and the Musselmans, Martins, Hoffmans, and Gingerichs to settle in the area. Wallace sold the Germany Company 45,185 acres of land at $1.00 an acre.

In 1834, Edward Bristow became one of Elmira's first settlers when he purchased 53 acres of land here for 50 cents per acre. A community by the name of Bristow's Corners was in existence in 1839 when a post office was assigned there. In 1853 the community was renamed Elmira. In the 1850s, German settlers moved into the community, including Oswald, Esche, Steffen and Tresinger. Like most of the township, the primary settlers in the Elmira area were Mennonites who still form a significant proportion of the population today. The town still retains much of its traditional Pennsylvania Dutch character.

Table of Contents

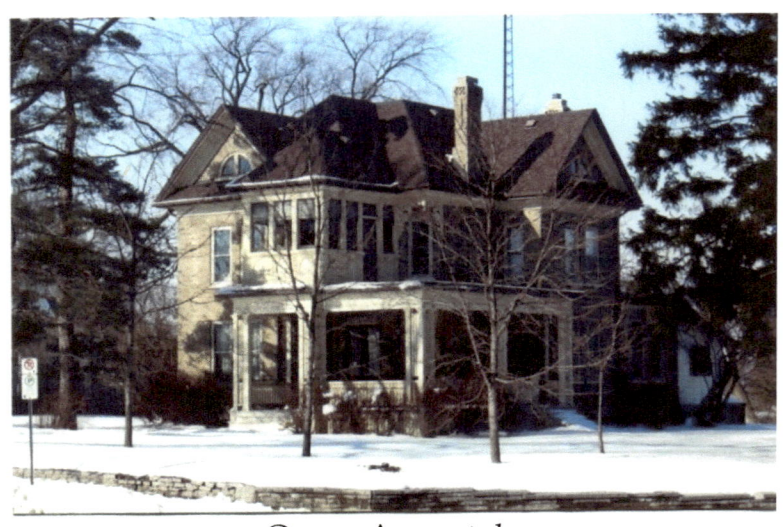

Queen Anne style

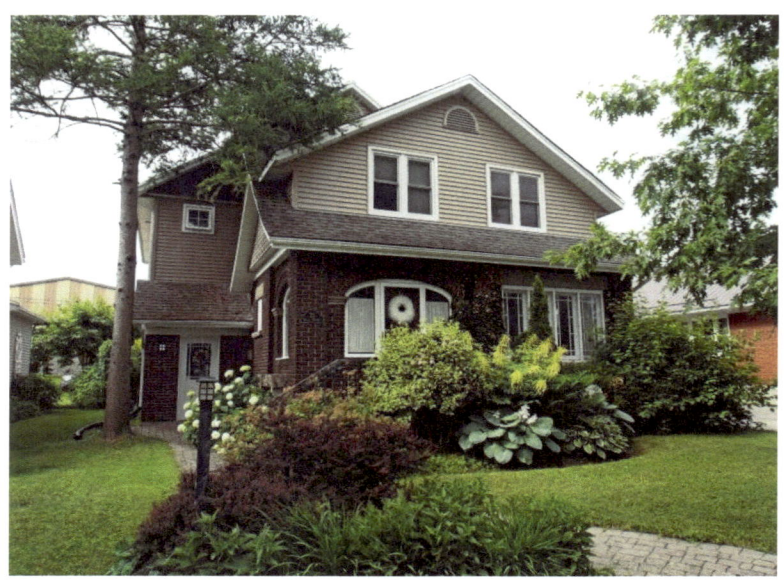

23 South Street

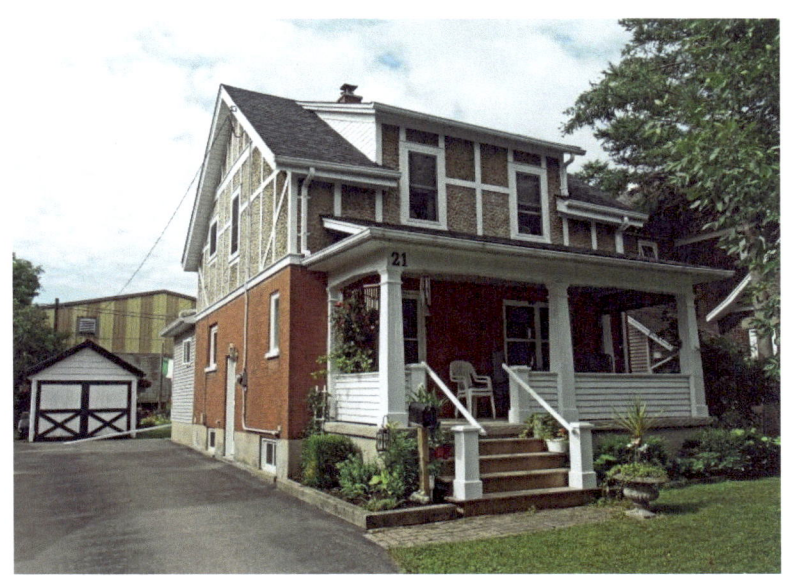

21 South Street – Tudor style

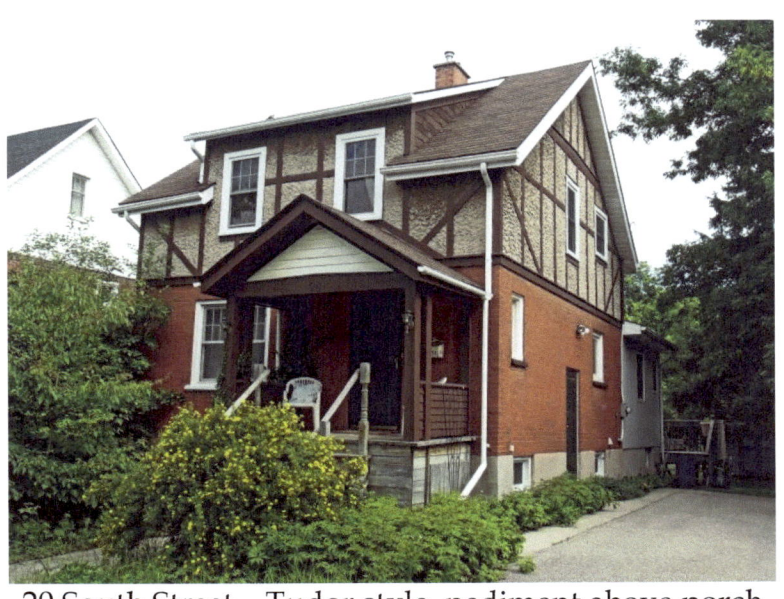

20 South Street – Tudor style, pediment above porch

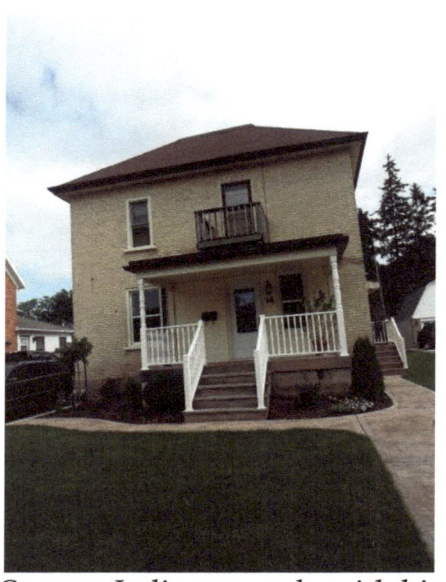

14 South Street – Italianate style with hipped roof

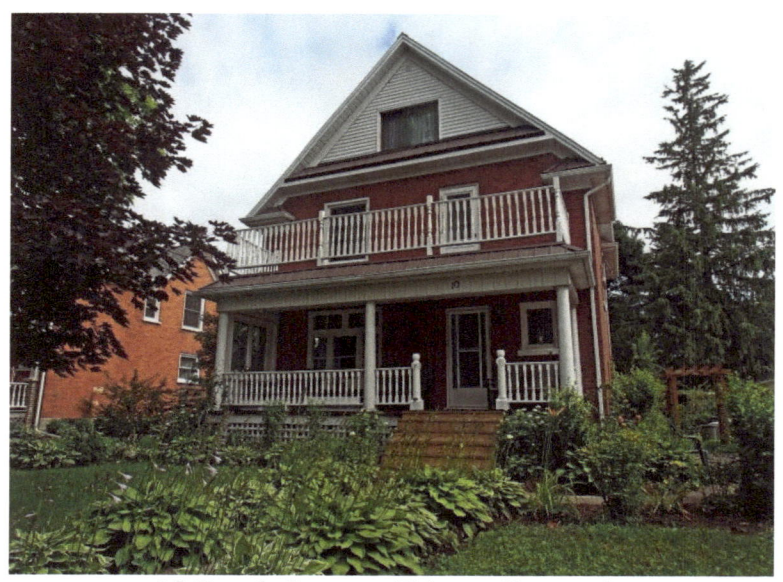

10 South Street – Edwardian style

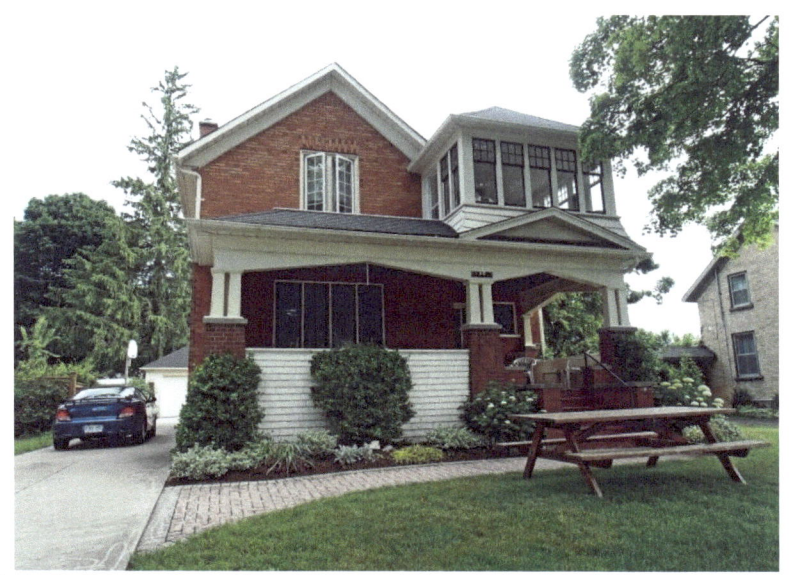

8 South Street – enclosed sunroom on second floor, pediment above verandah

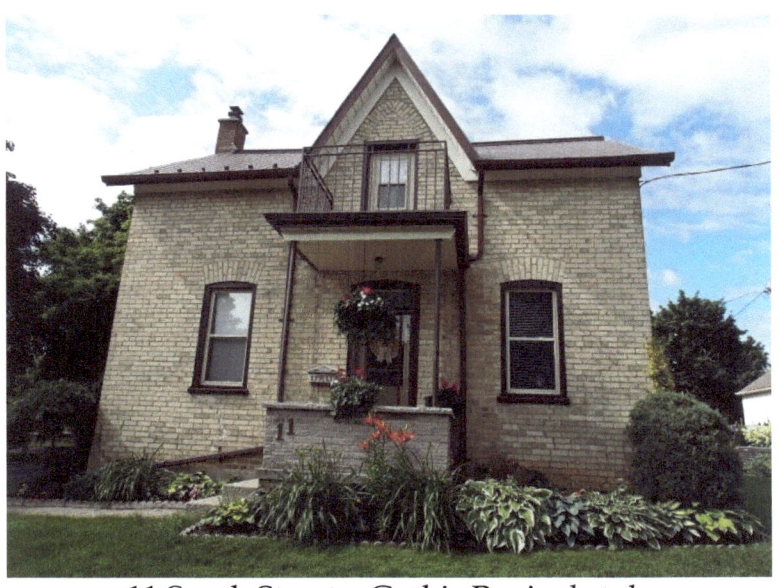

11 South Street – Gothic Revival style

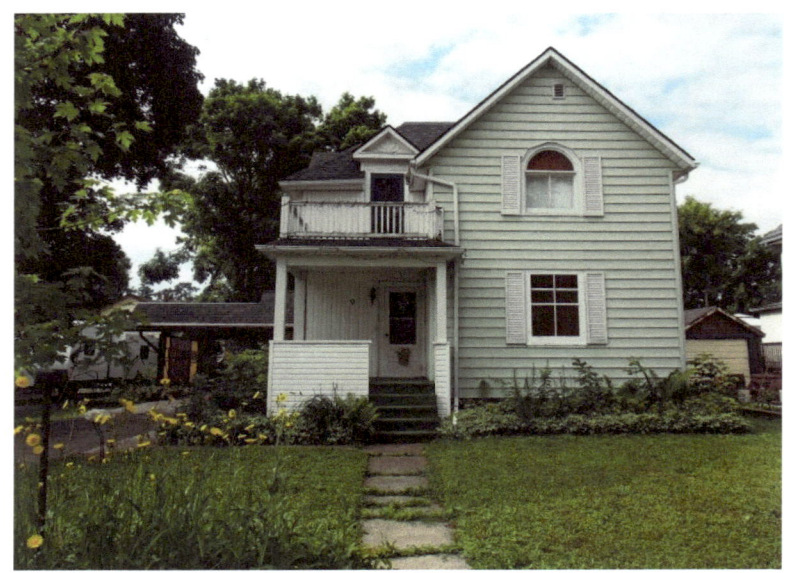

9 South Street – Gothic Revival

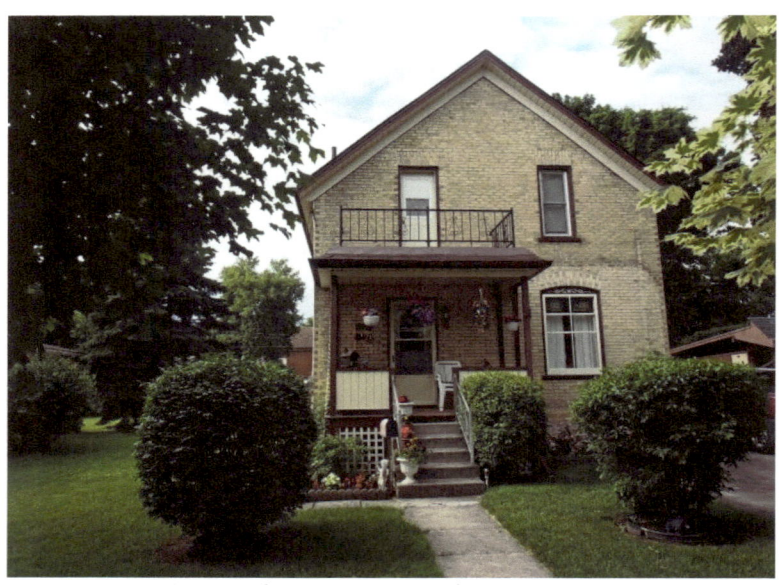

7 South Street – Gothic Revival

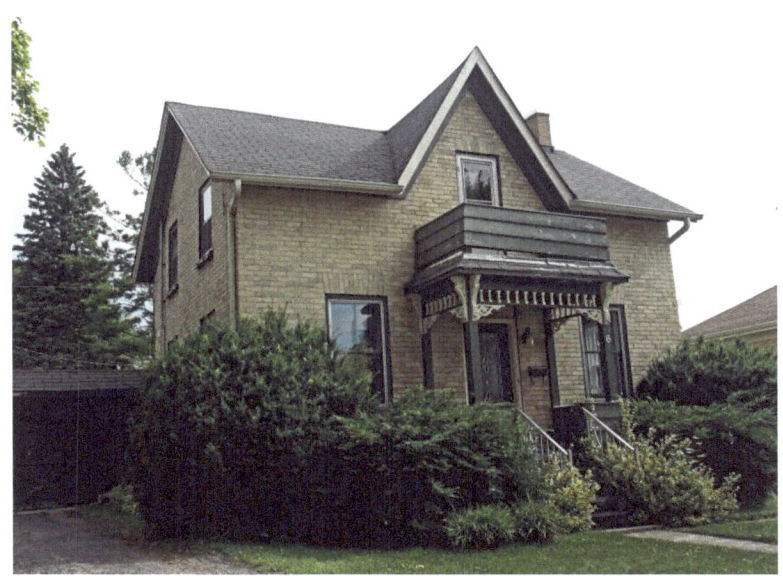

6 South Street – Gothic Revival

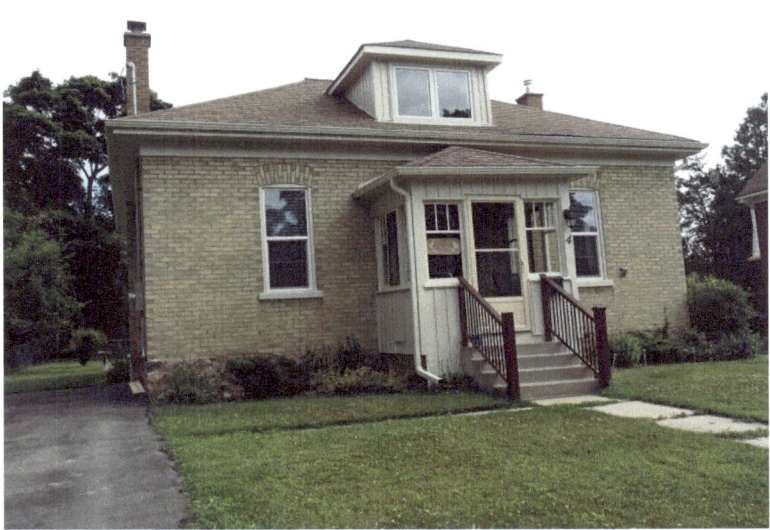

4 South Street – one storey Italianate style with dormer in hipped roof

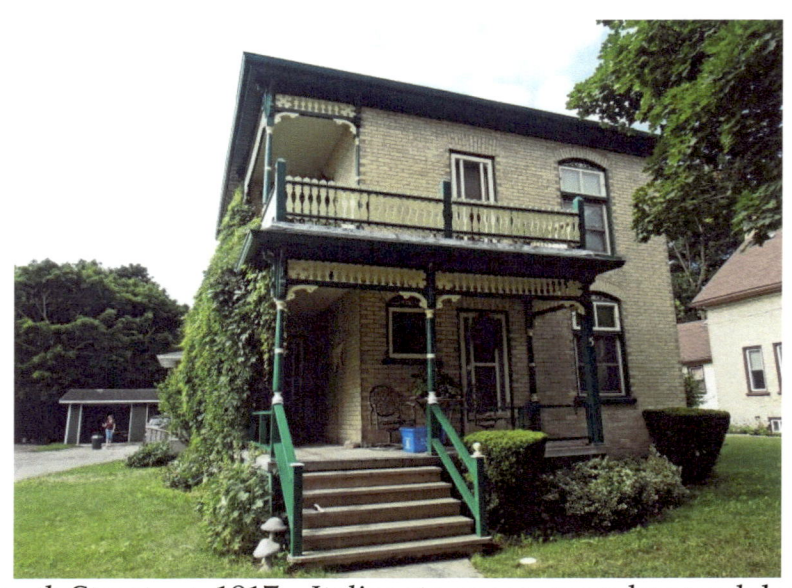

5 South Street – c. 1917 – Italianate, wraparound verandahs on both storeys

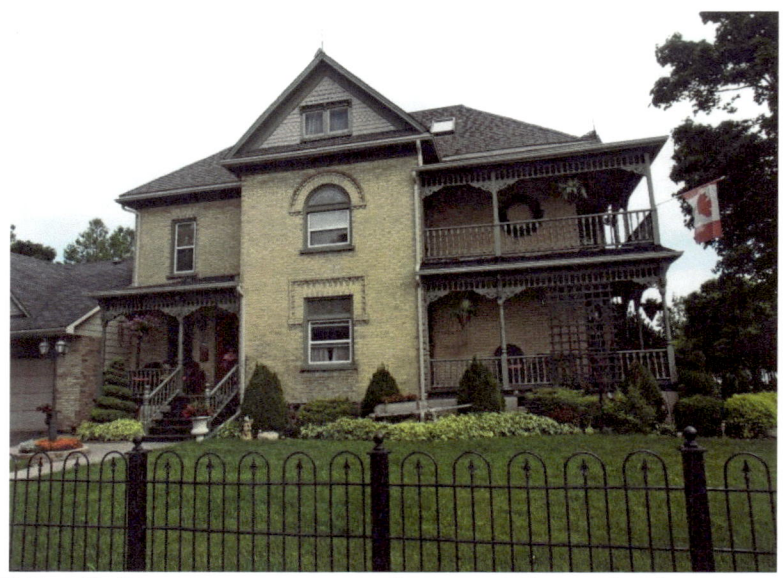

2 South Street - wraparound verandahs on both storeys

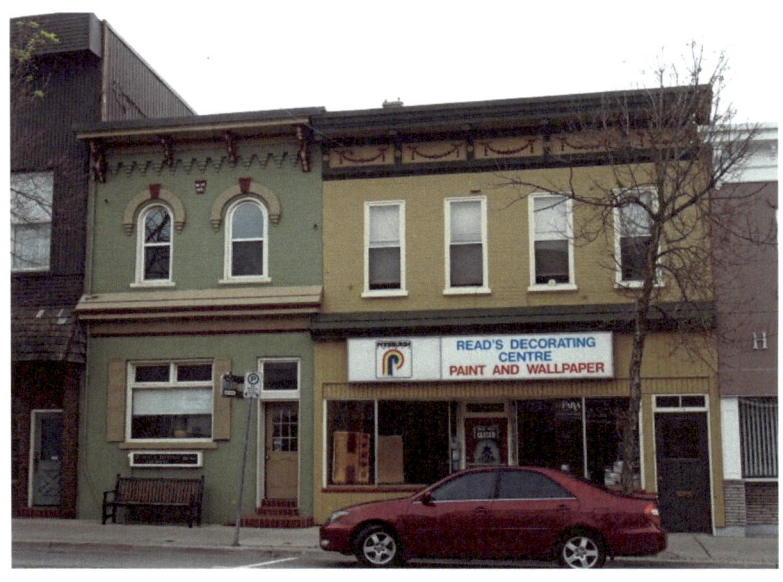

Arthur Street South – arched window voussoirs with keystones

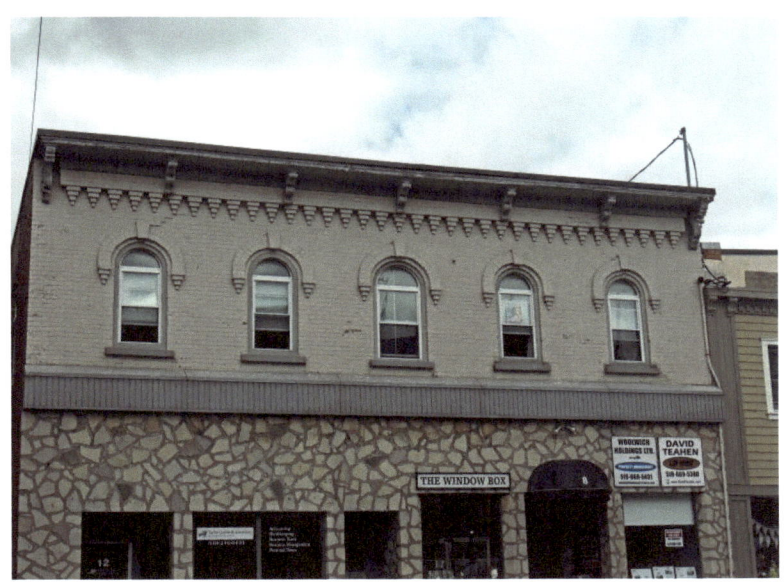

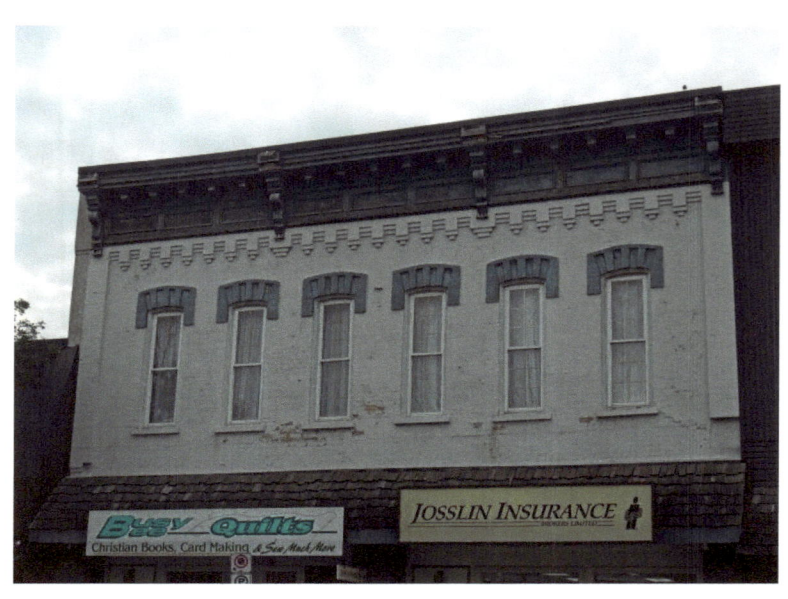

Arthur Street South

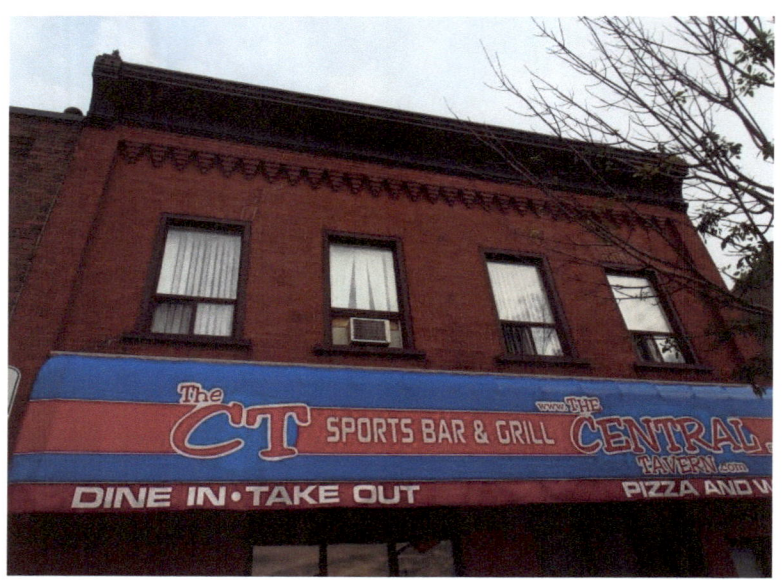

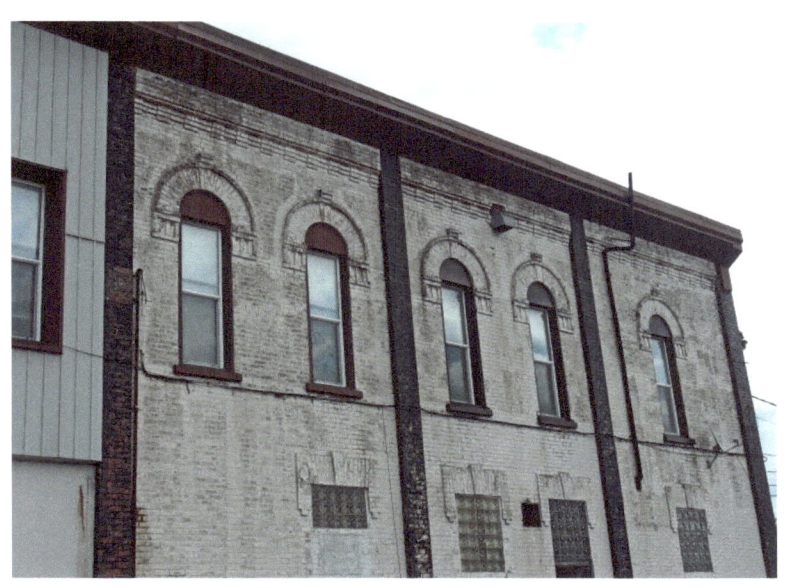

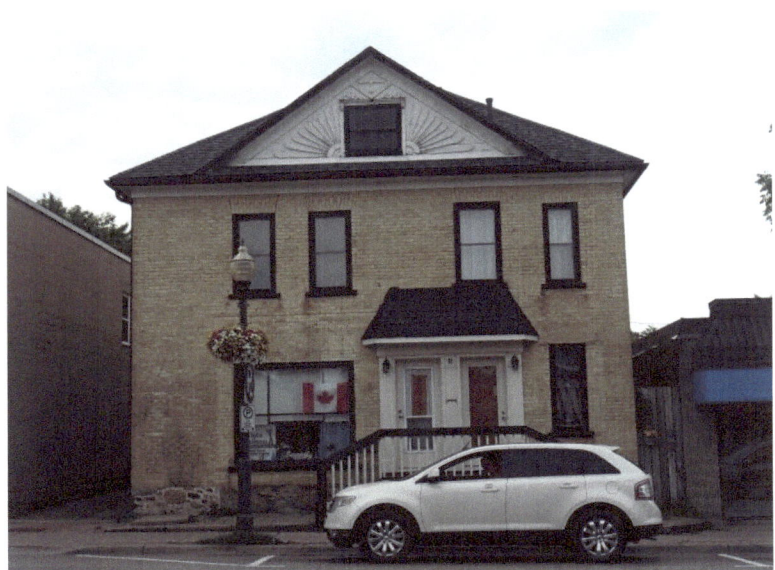

51 Arthur Street South

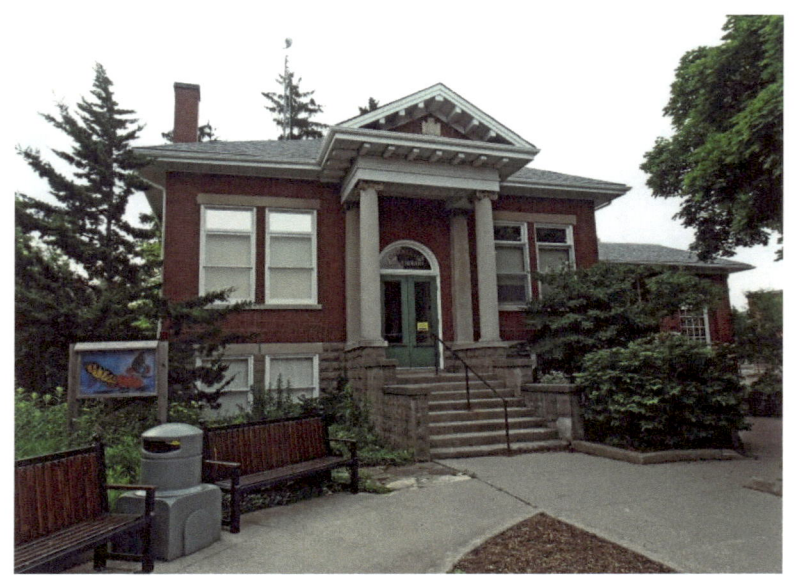

Carnegie Free Library - In 1911, the Elmira Library received a Carnegie grant after being supported by the local businesses for many years.

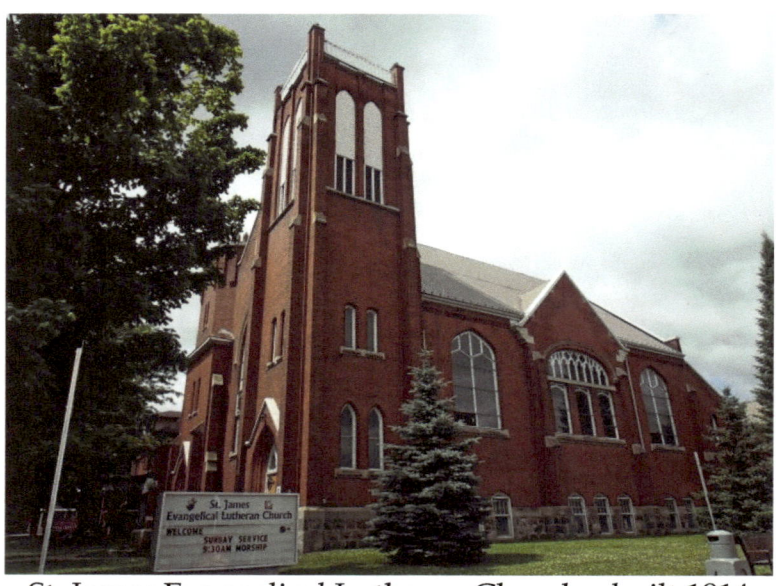

St. James Evangelical Lutheran Church – built 1914

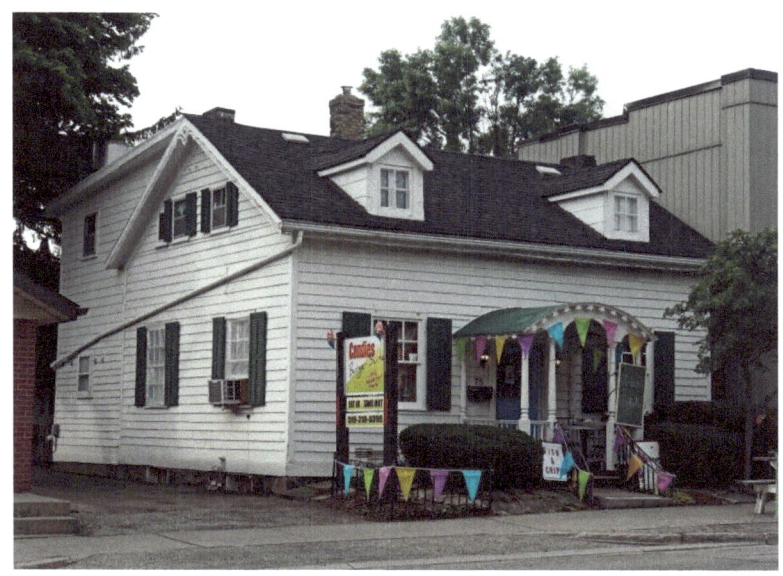

75 Arthur Street South – dormers in attic

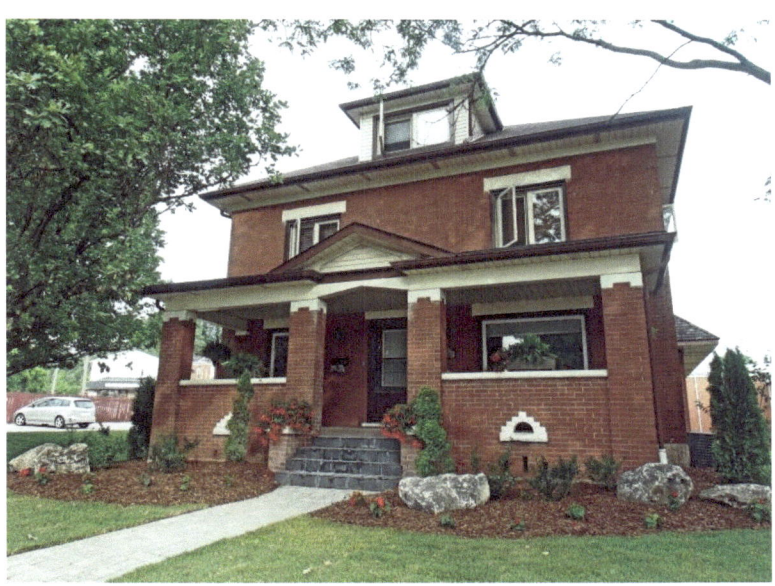

62 Arthur Street South – Italianate – dormer in attic

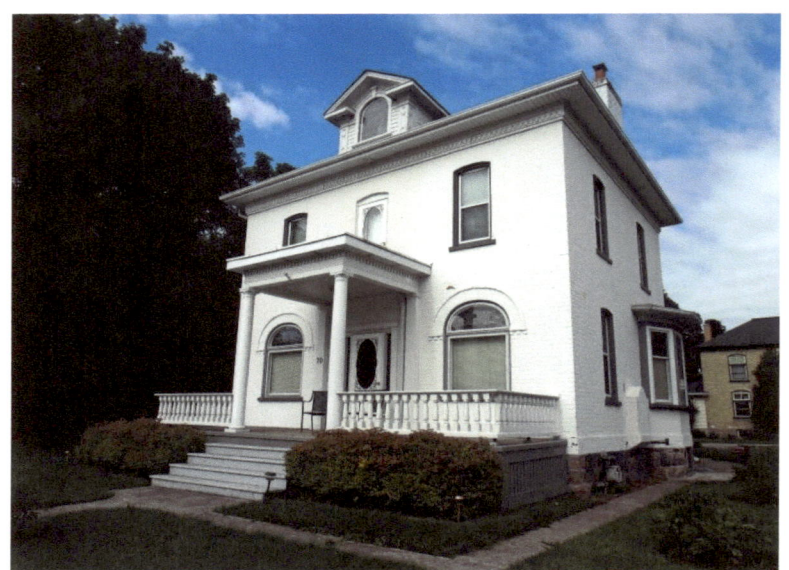

70 Arthur Street South – Italianate – dormer in attic

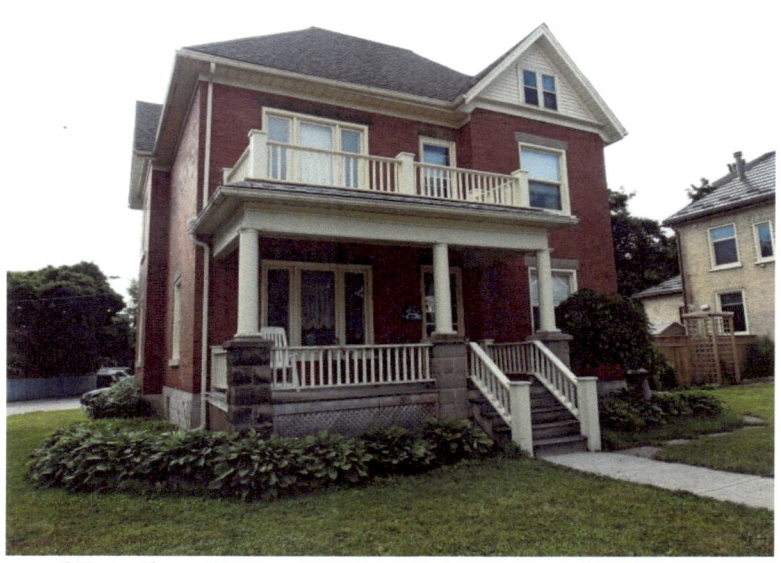

97 Arthur Street South – Edwardian/Italianate

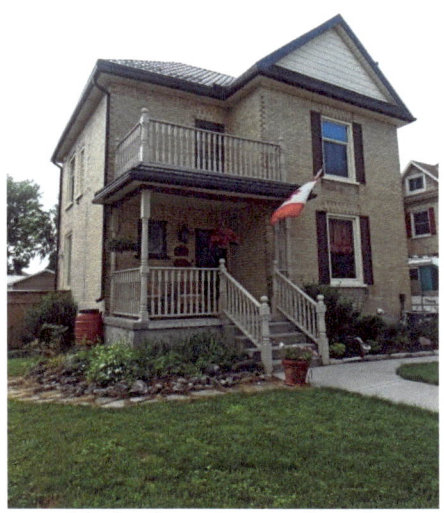

99 Arthur Street South

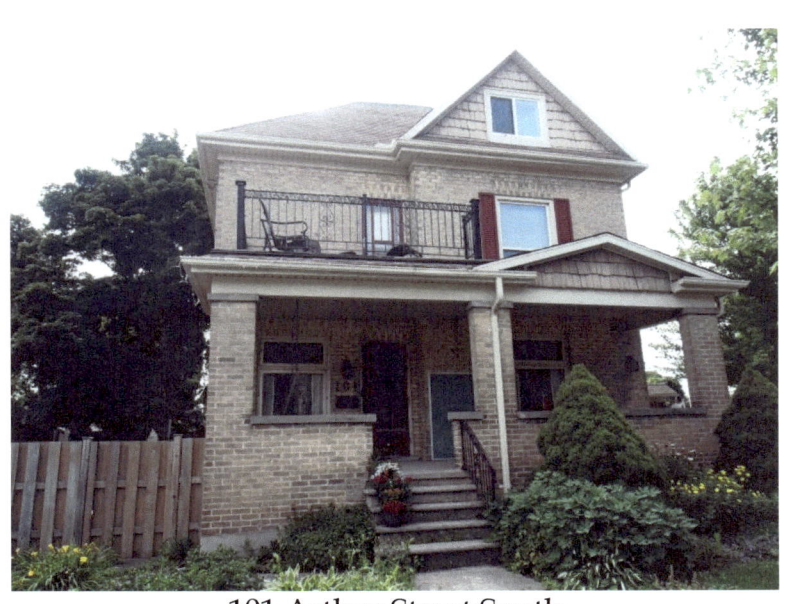

101 Arthur Street South

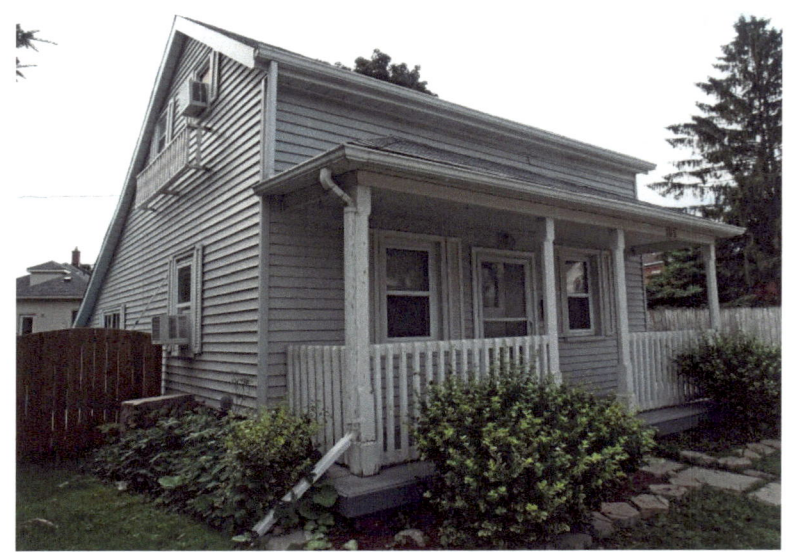

103 Arthur Street South

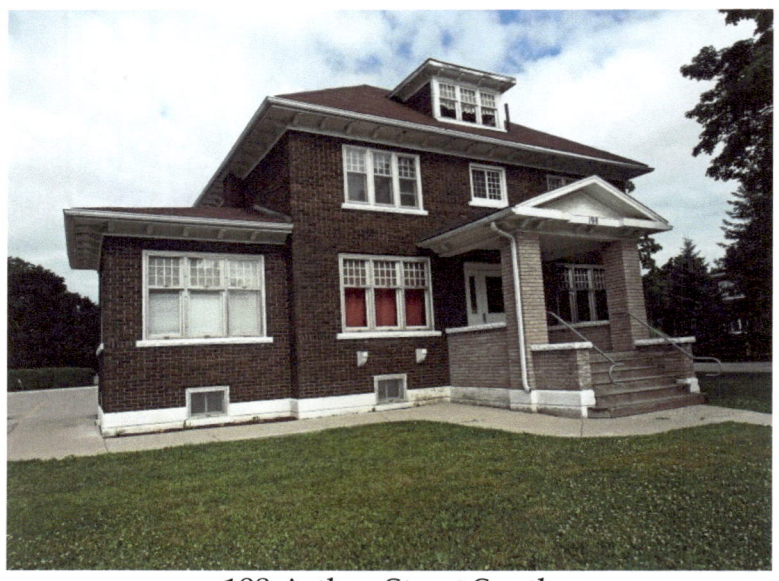

198 Arthur Street South

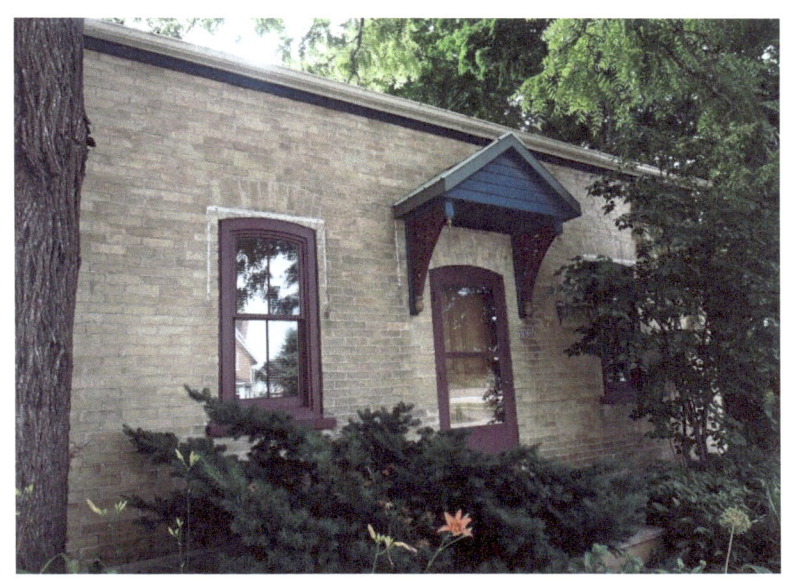

113 Arthur Street South

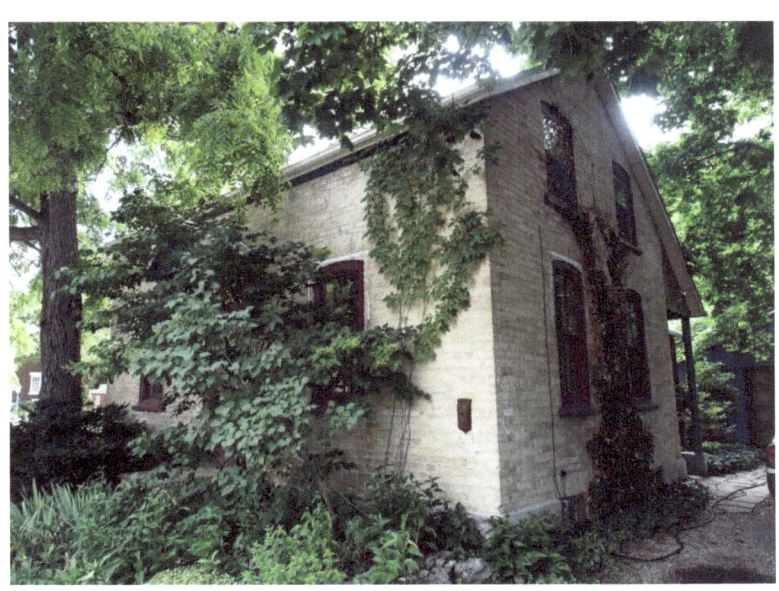

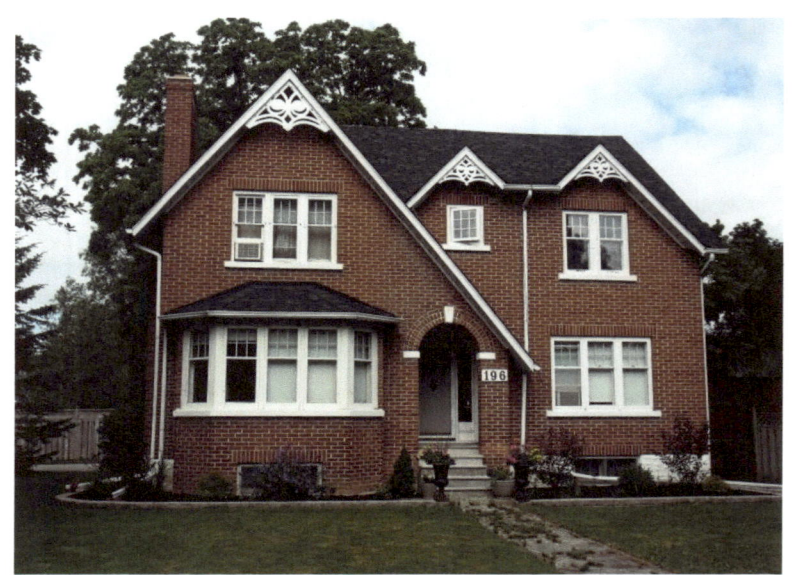

196 Arthur Street South – Gothic Revival, Vergeboard trim

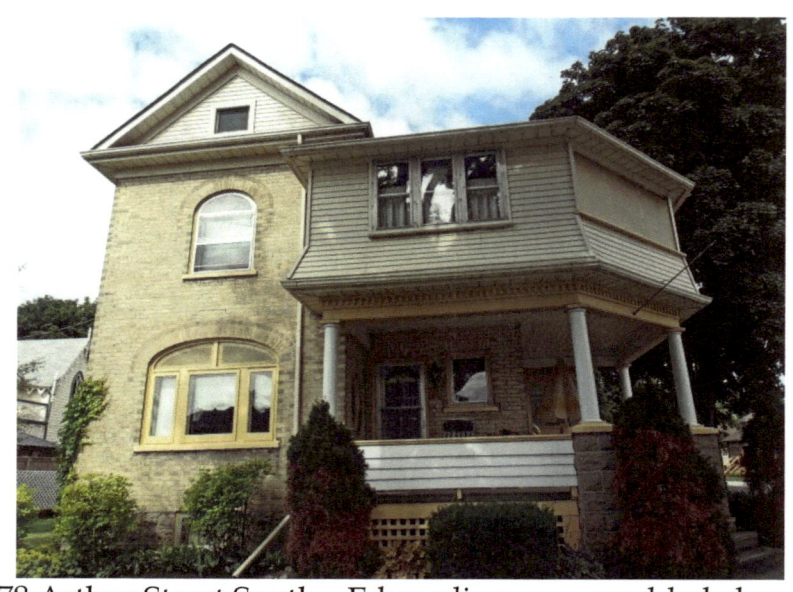

78 Arthur Street South – Edwardian – room added above wraparound verandah

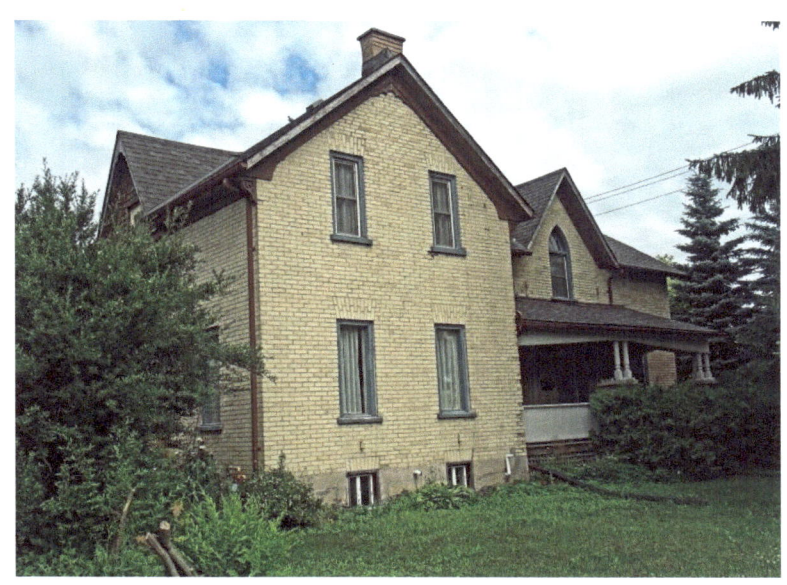

88 Arthur Street South – Gothic Revival

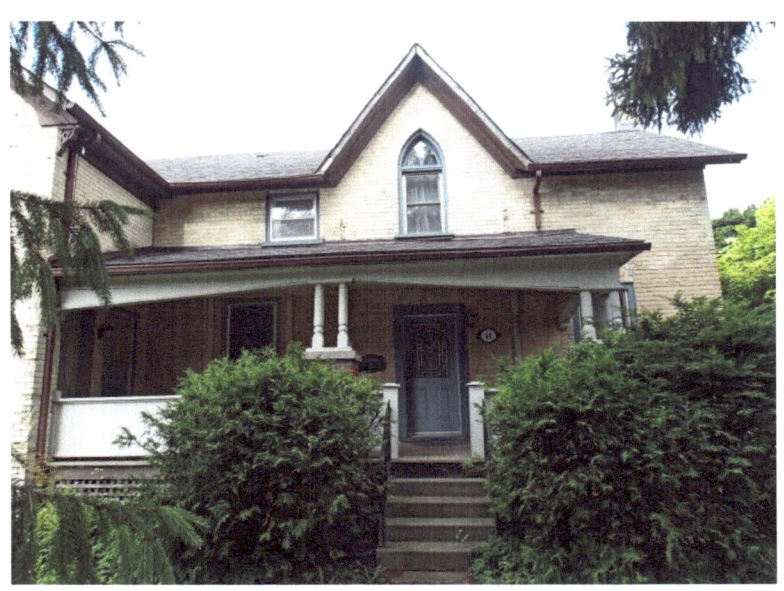

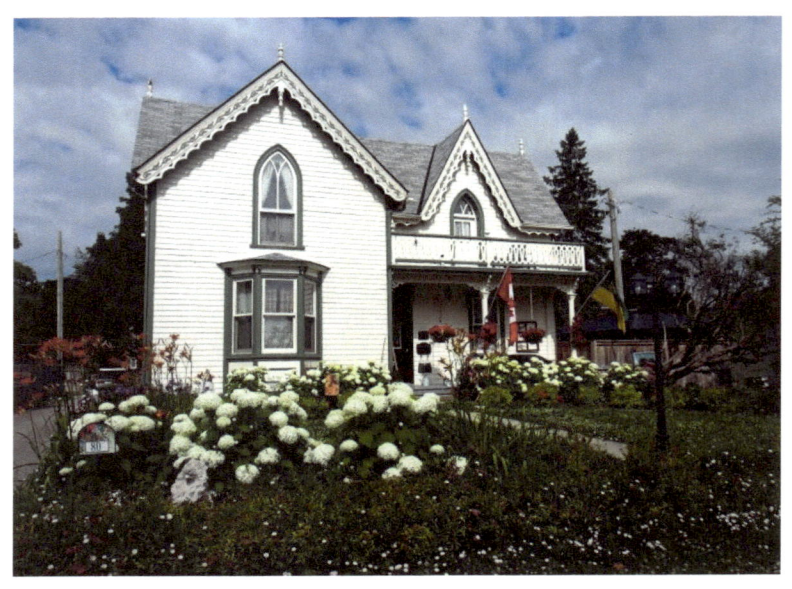

80 Arthur Street South – Gothic Revival, Vergeboard trim

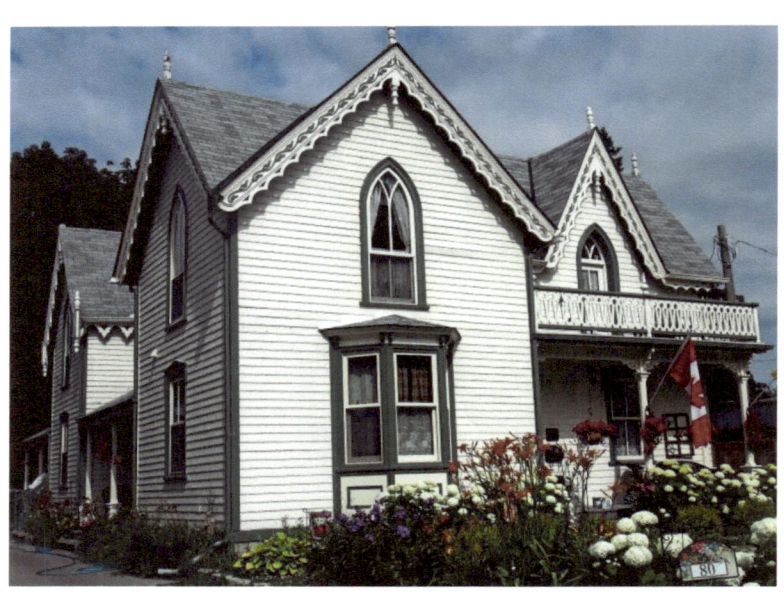

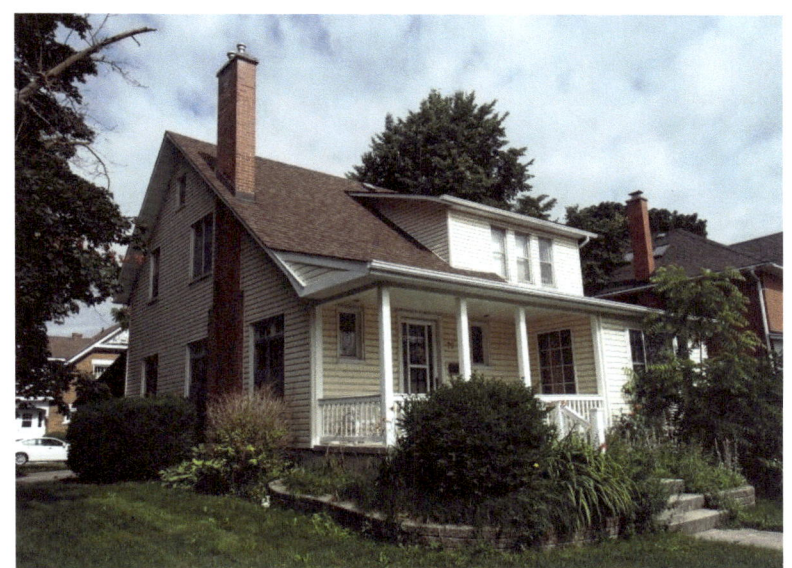

76 Arthur Street South

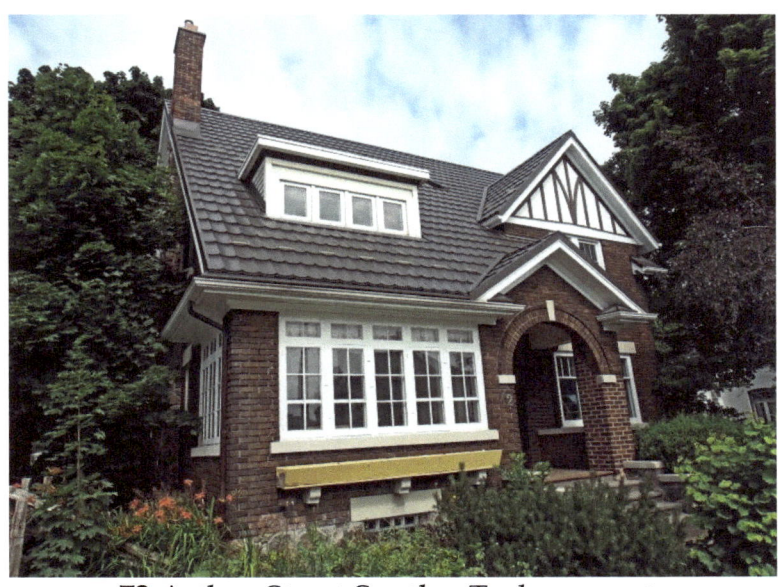

72 Arthur Street South – Tudor accents

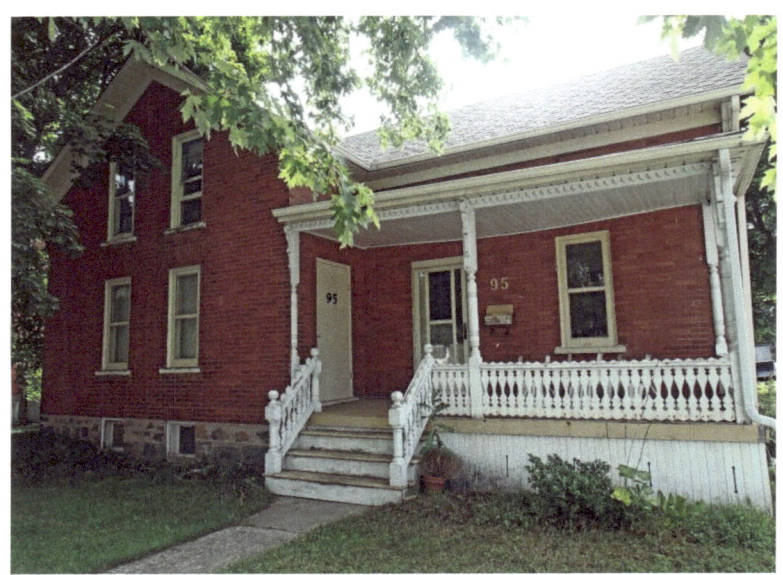

95 Arthur Street South

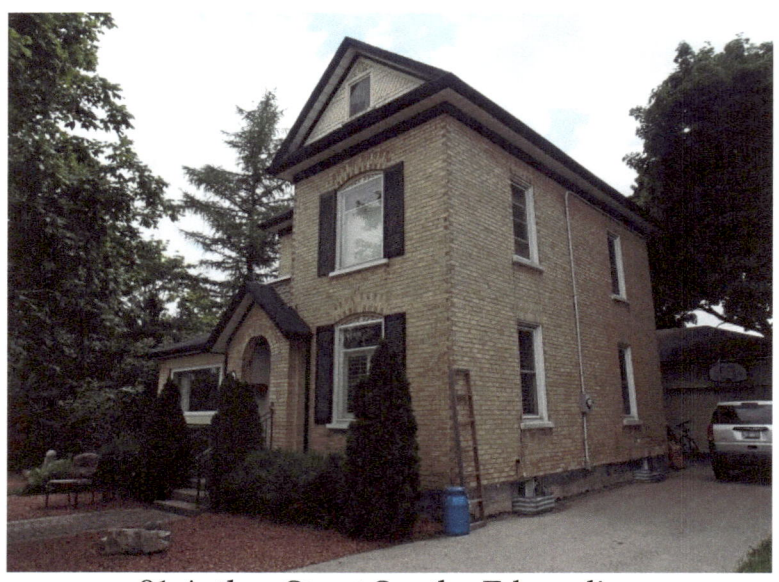

91 Arthur Street South - Edwardian

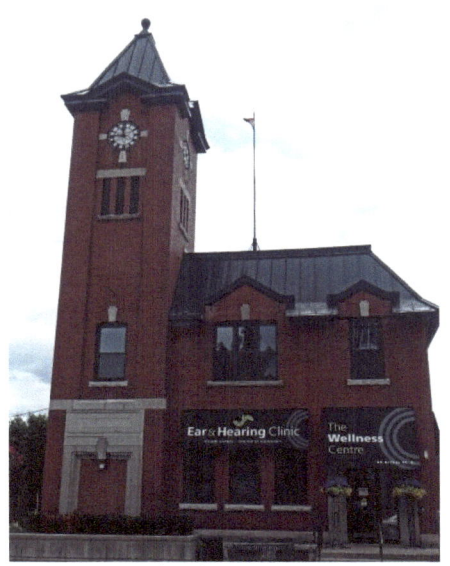

Clock Tower

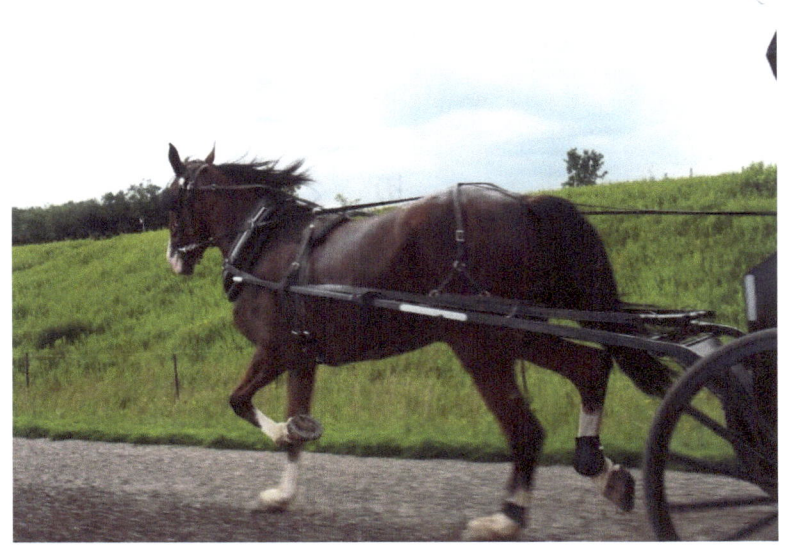

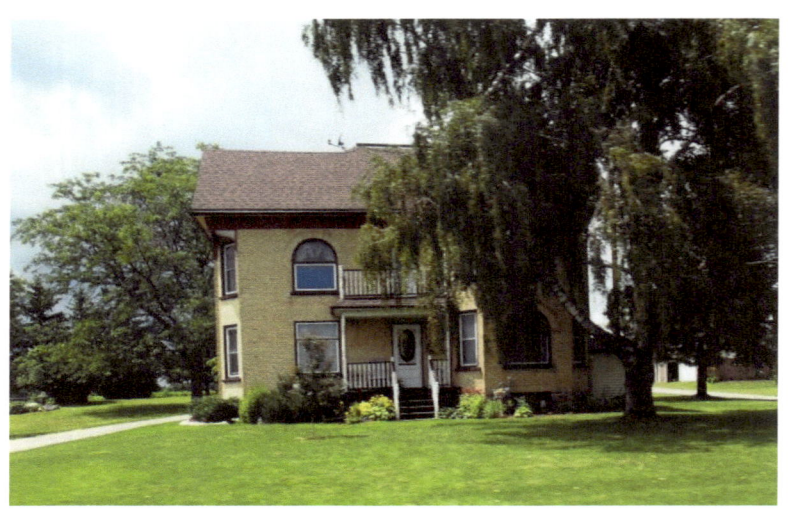

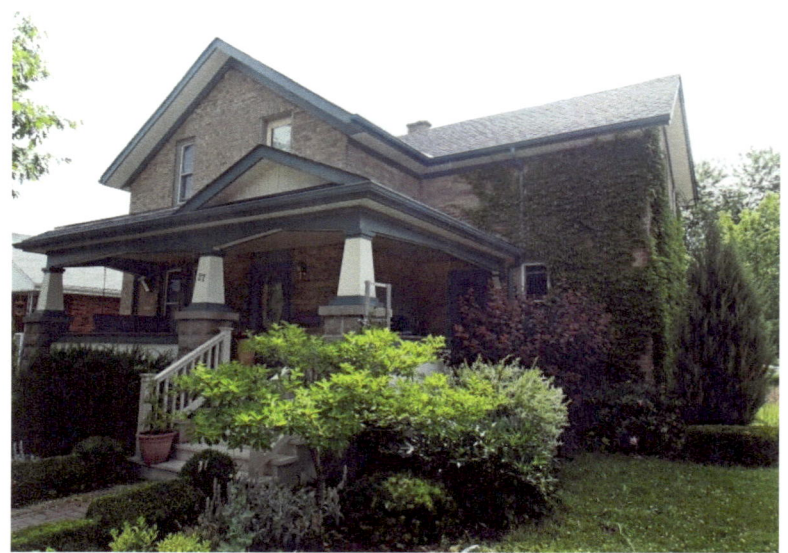

27 Queen Street

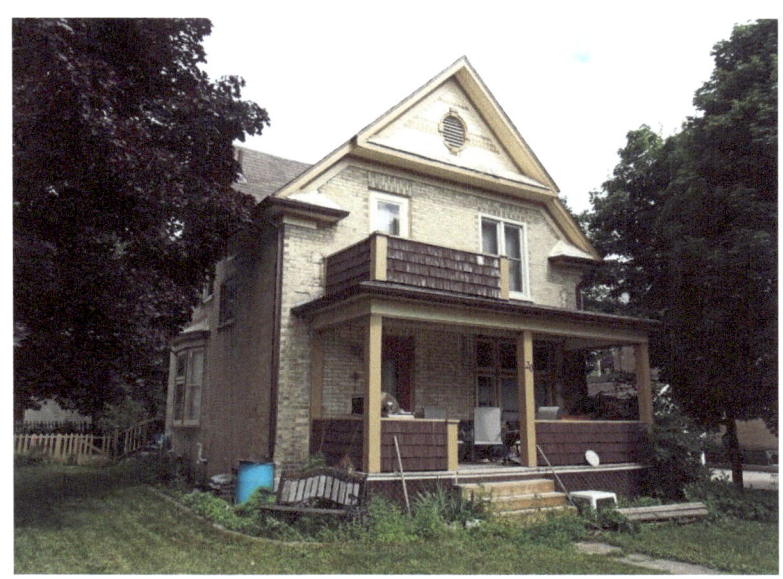

20 Queen Street - Edwardian

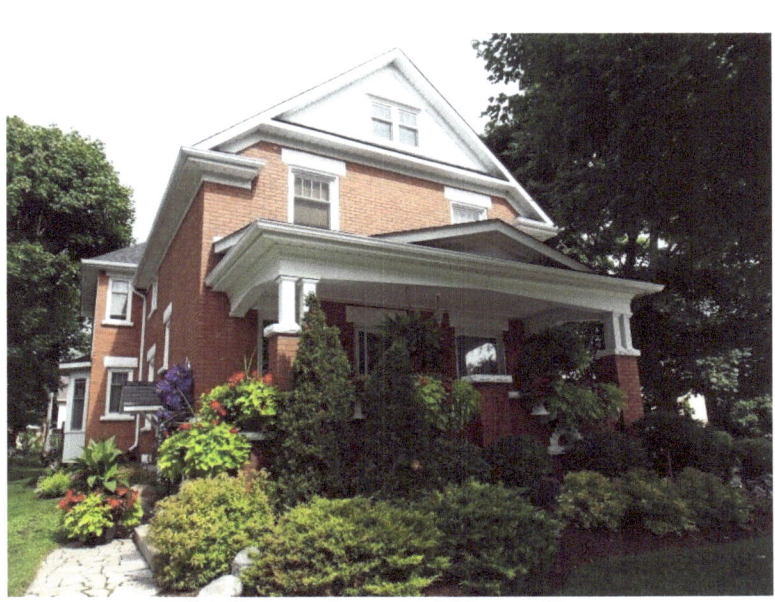

24 Queen Street – Edwardian

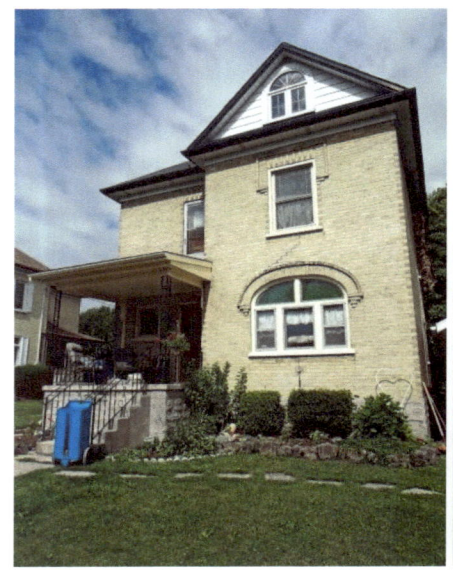

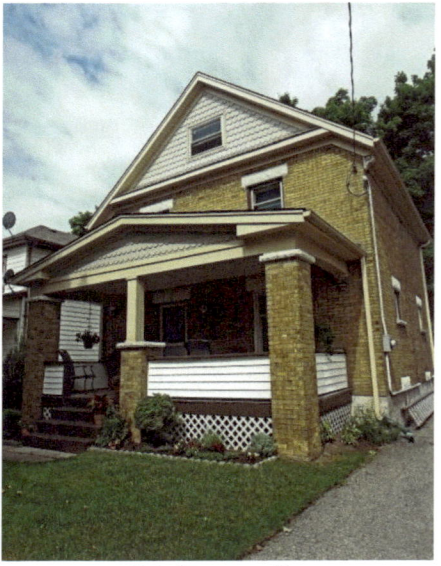

34 Queen Street
Edwardian with
pediment above verandah

Edwardian with Romanesque
style window arch

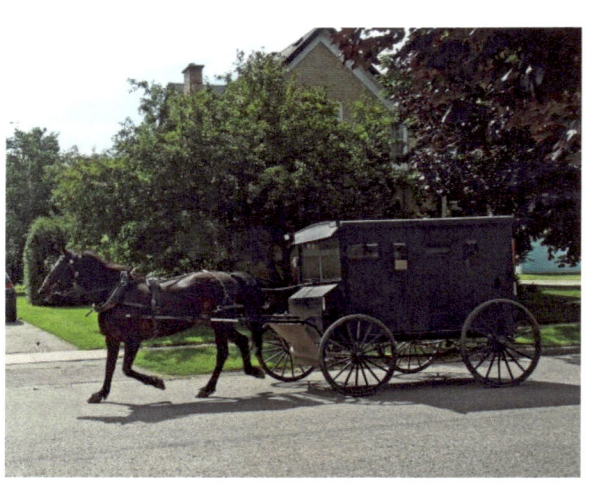

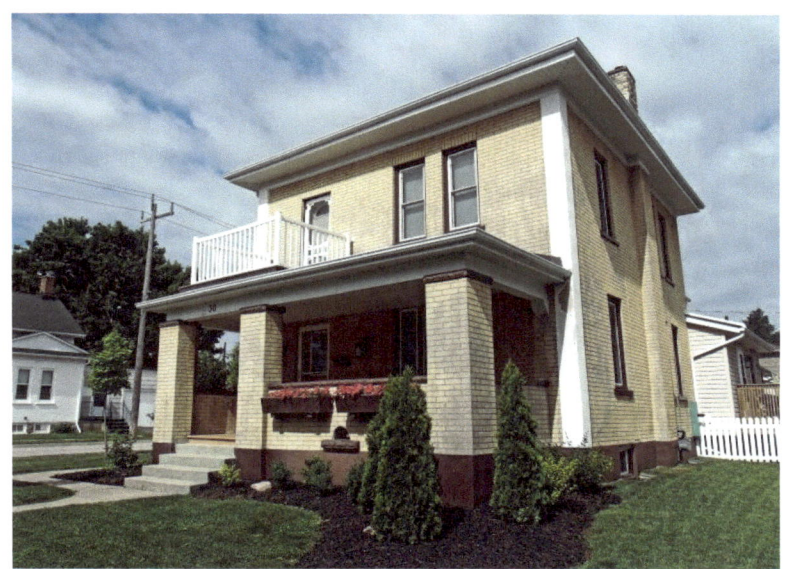

30 Queen Street – hip roof

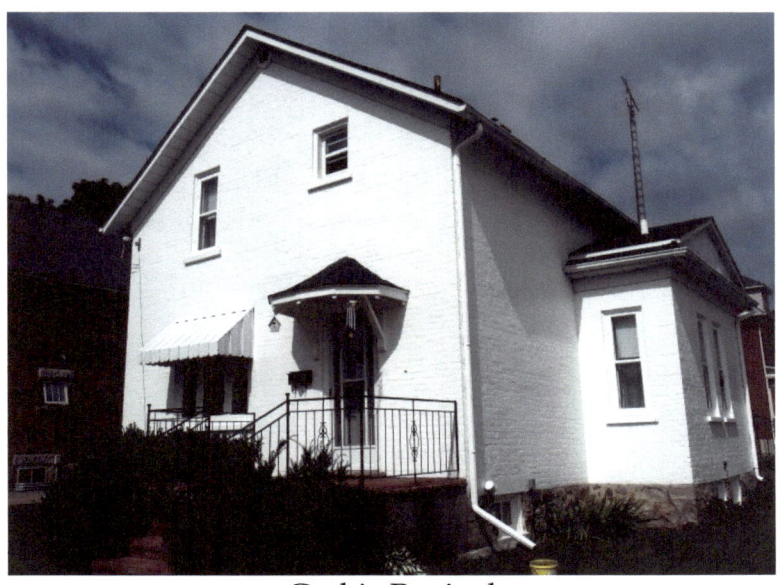

Gothic Revival

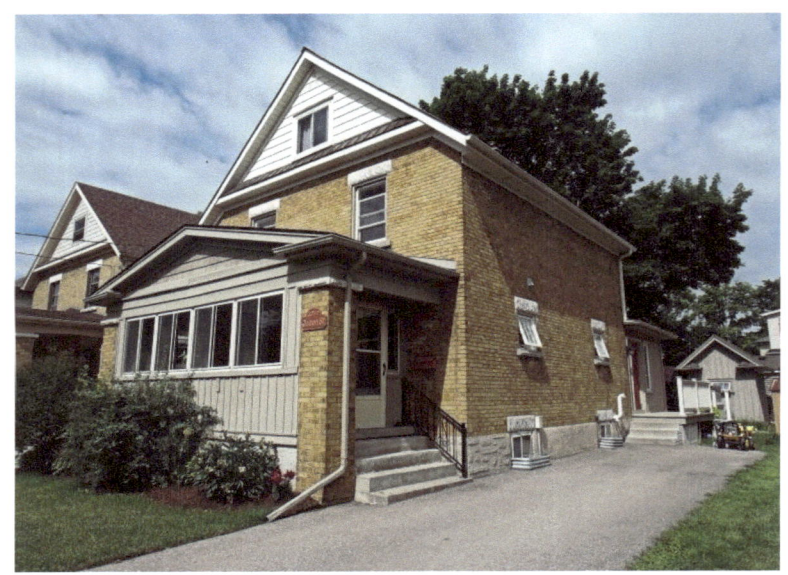

32 Queen Street - Edwardian

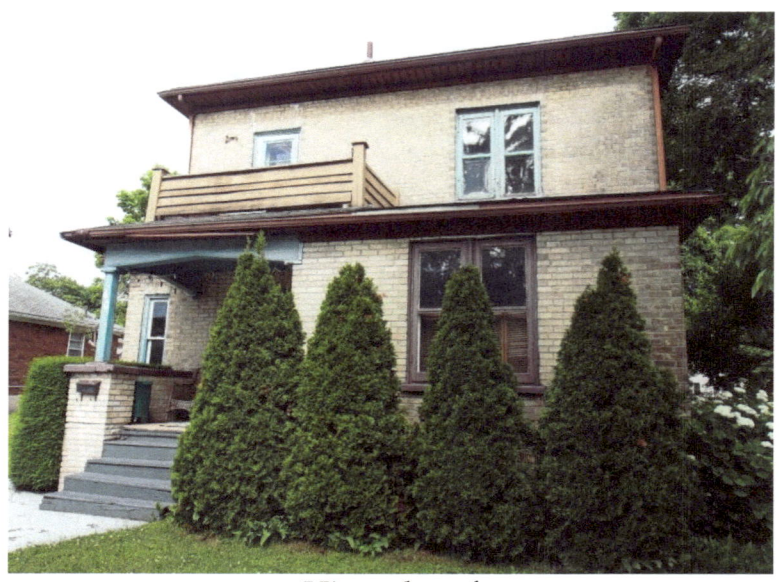

Hipped roof

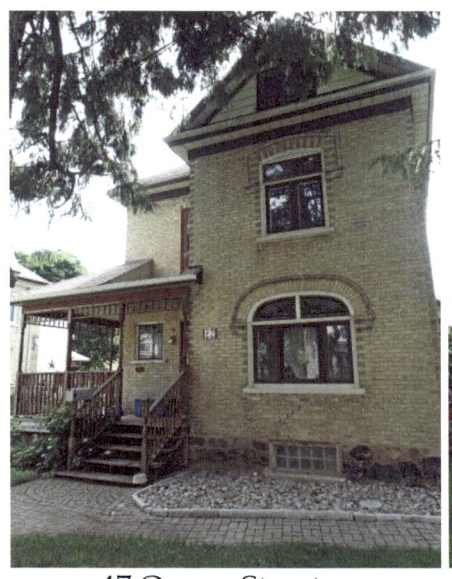

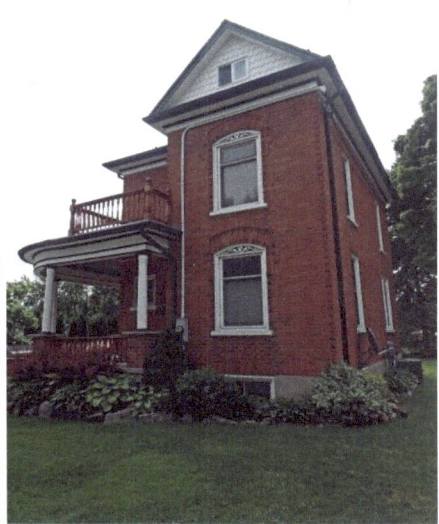

47 Queen Street   31 Queen Street

Edwardian

Romanesque style window arch

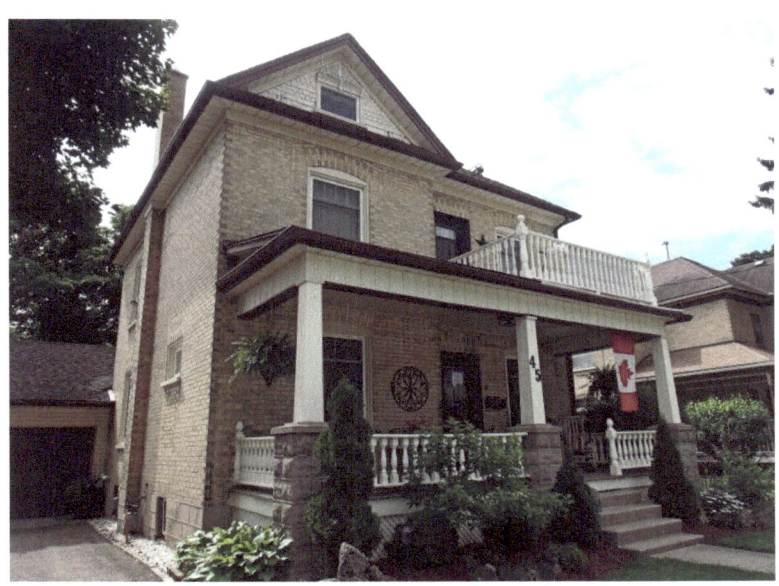

45 Queen Street - Edwardian

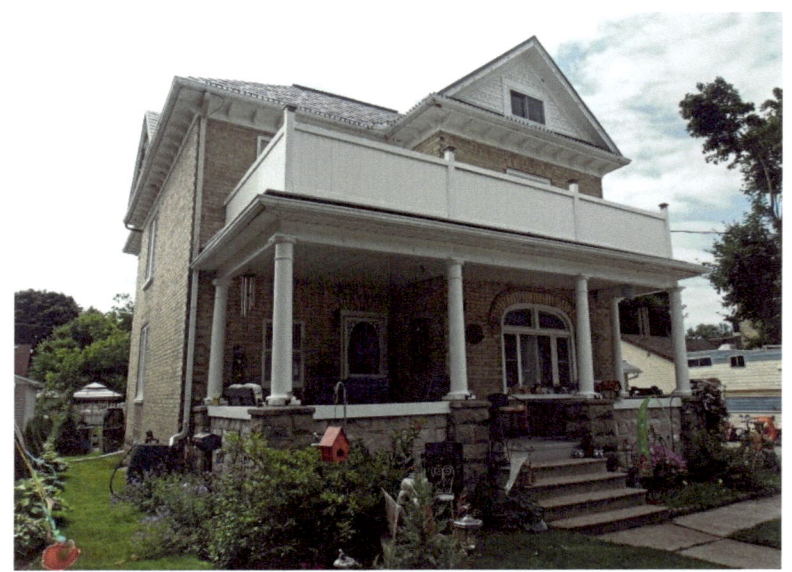

43 Queen Street - Romanesque style window arch on bottom right window

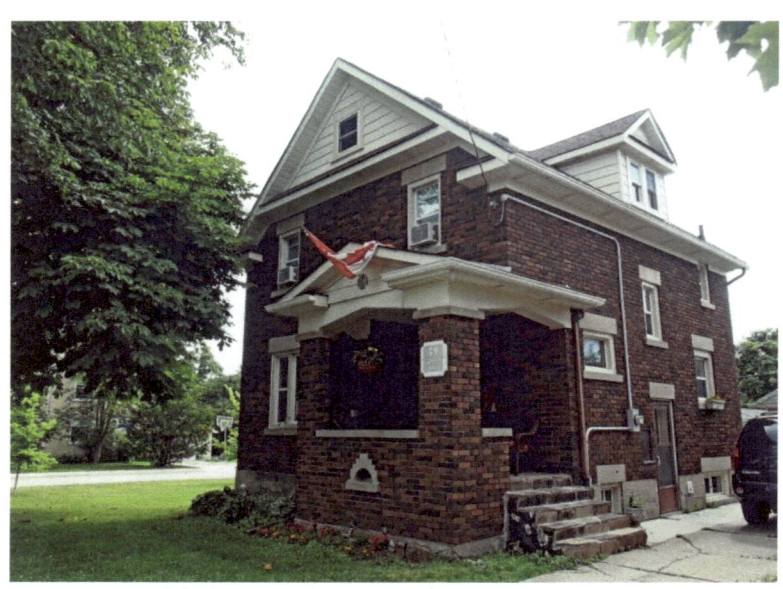

39 Queen Street – dormer in attic

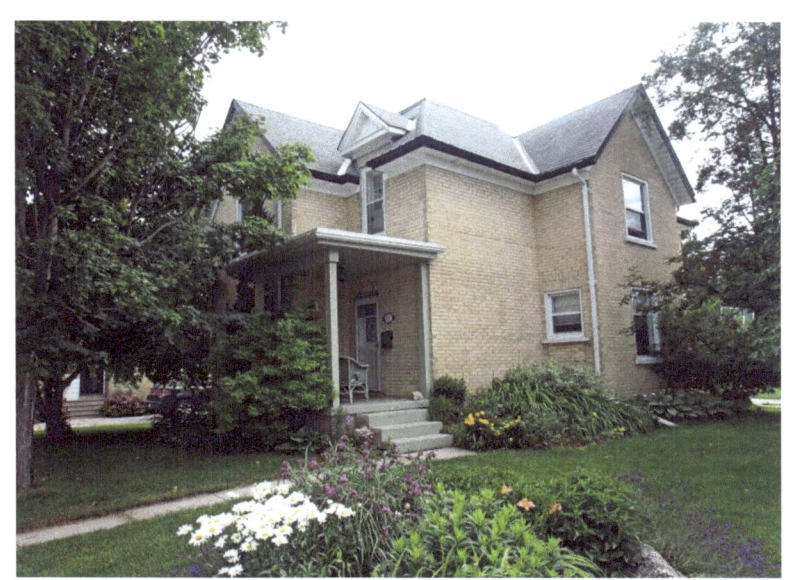

37 Queen Street – Gothic Revival

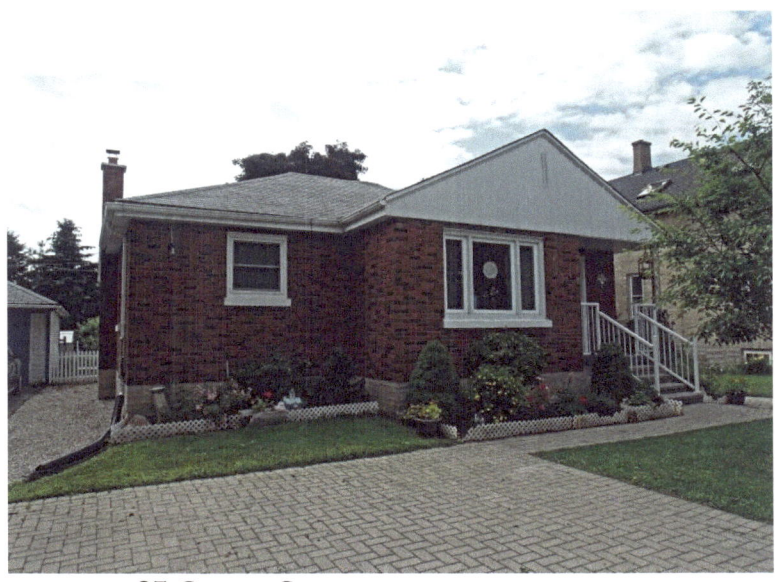

25 Queen Street – one storey cottage

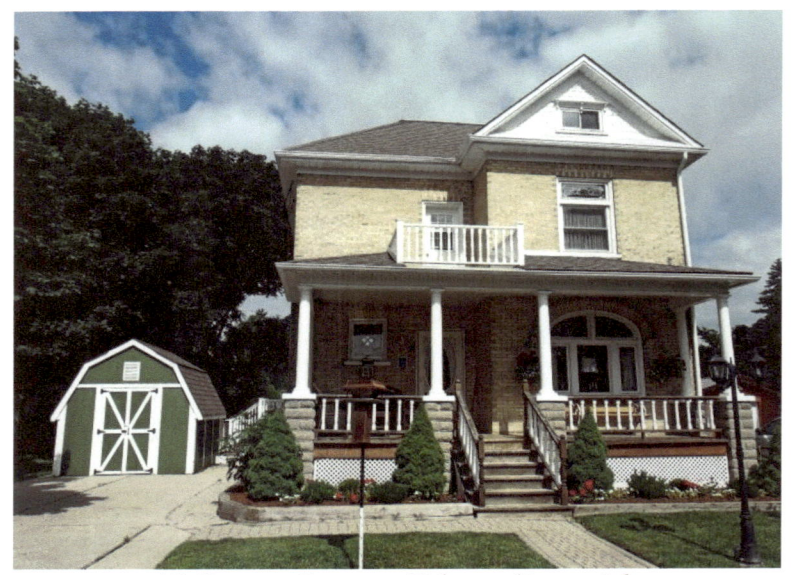

18 Queen Street – Edwardian with
Romanesque style window arch

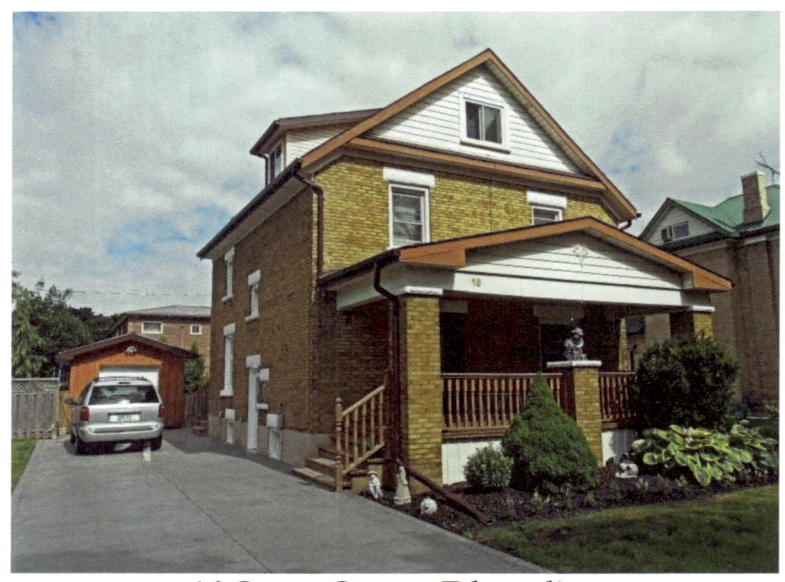

16 Queen Street - Edwardian

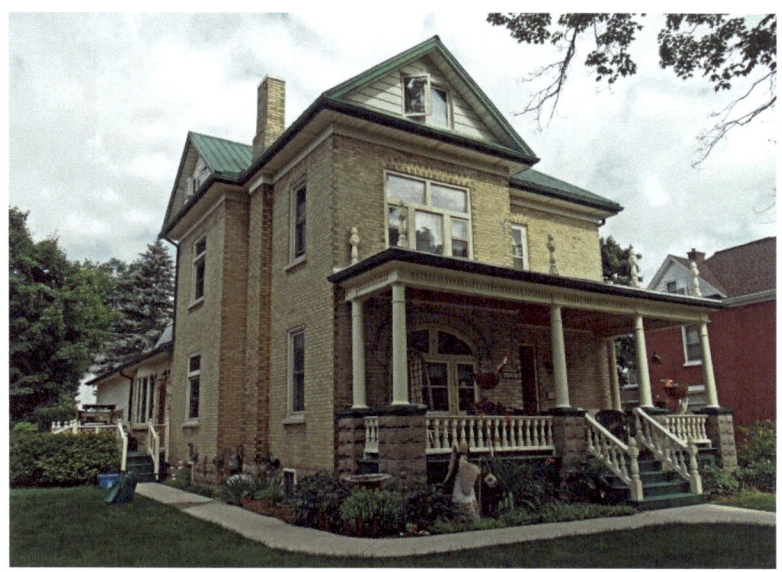

14 Queen Street - Edwardian with
Romanesque style window arch

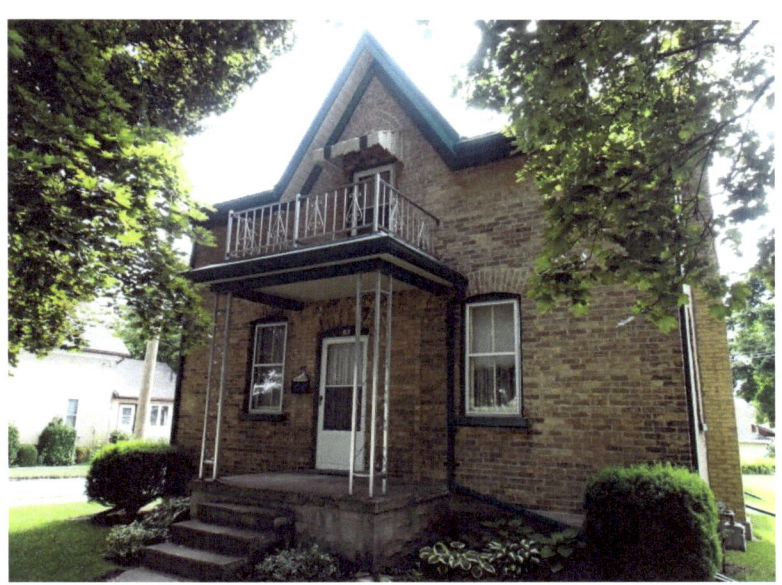

15 Queen Street – Gothic Revival

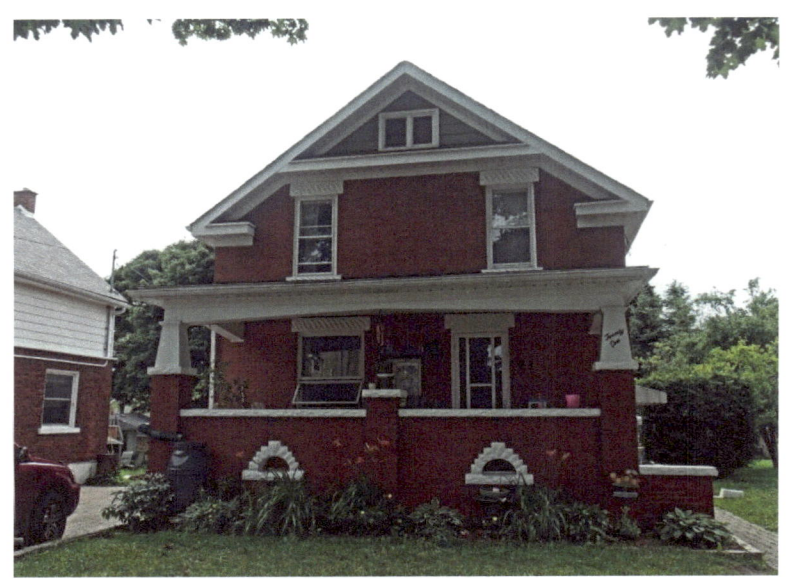

21 Queen Street – Edwardian, cornice return

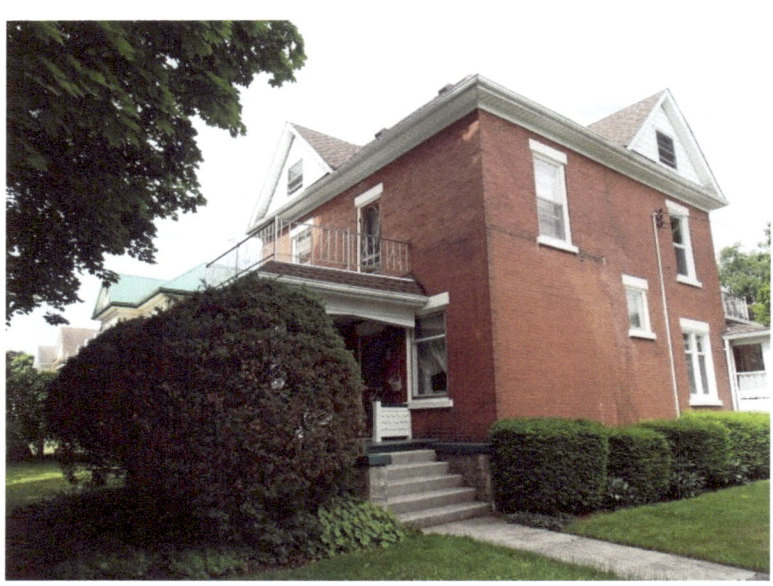

12 Queen Street

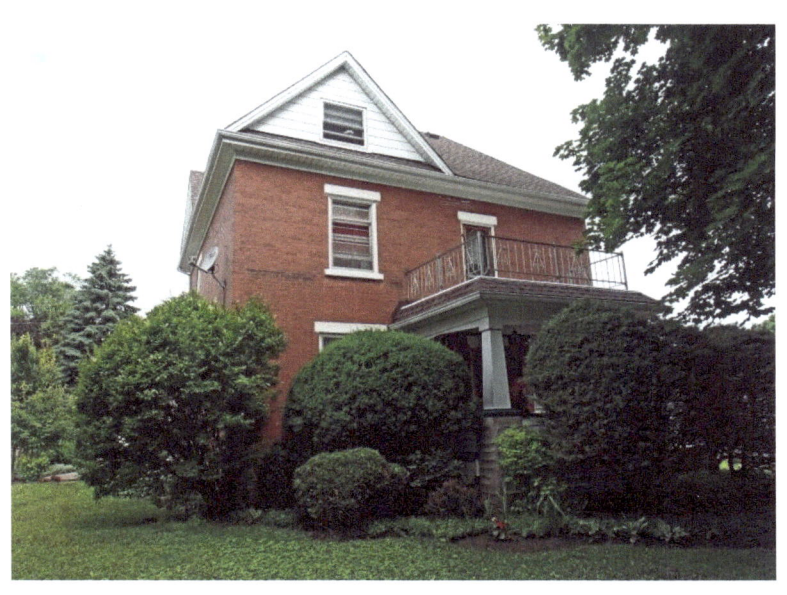

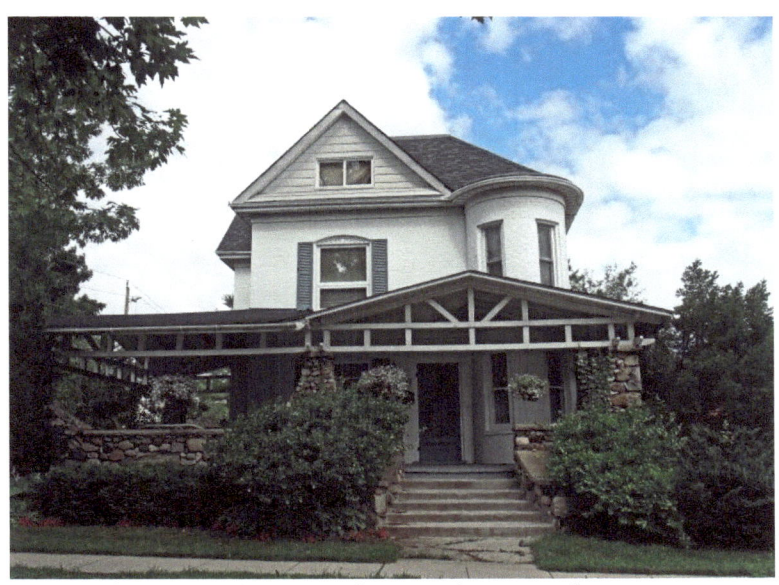

10 Queen Street – Queen Anne style, turret

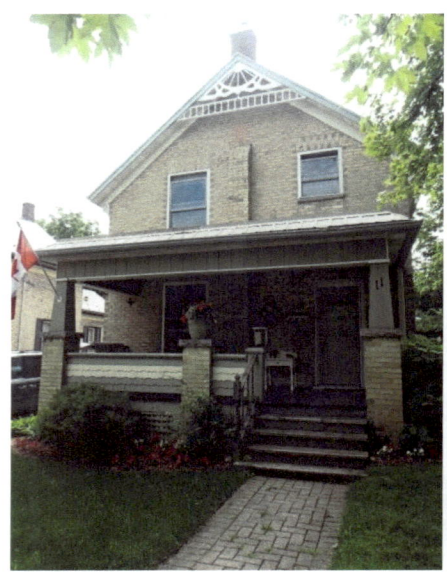 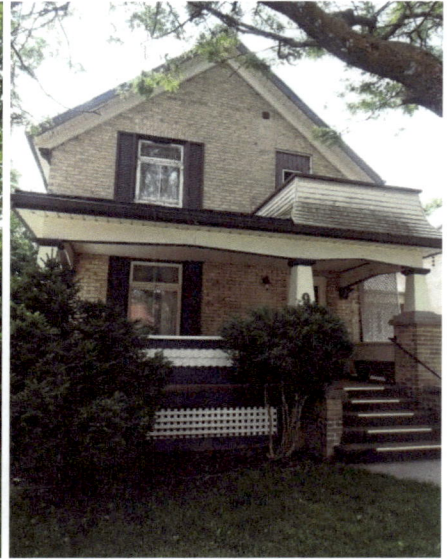

11 Queen Street   9 Queen Street

Gothic Revival

Vergeboard trim on gable

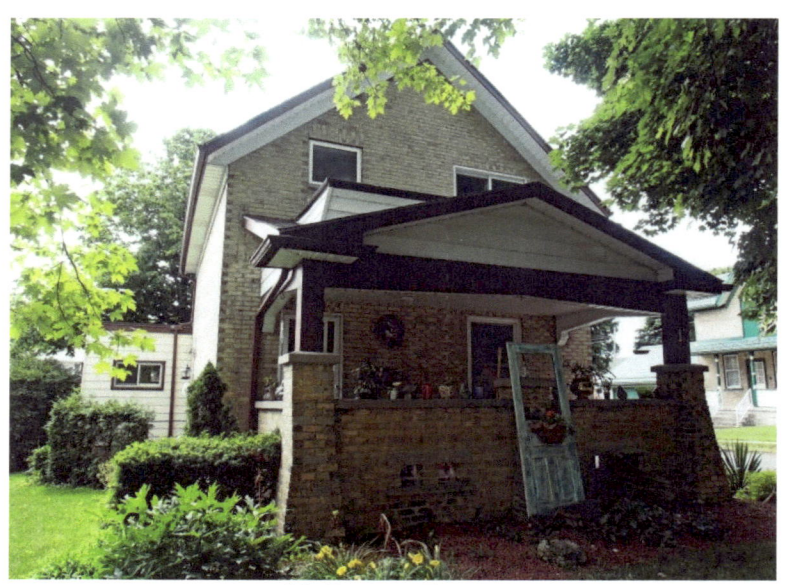

13 Queen Street

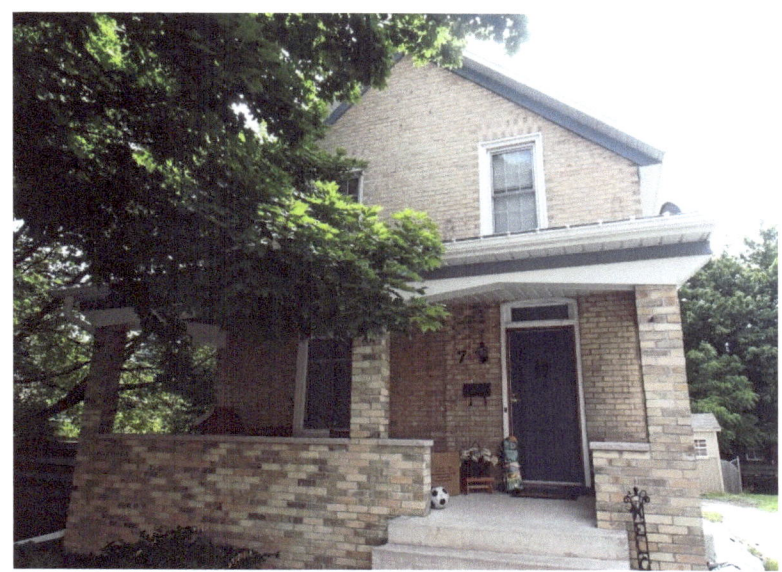

7 Queen Street

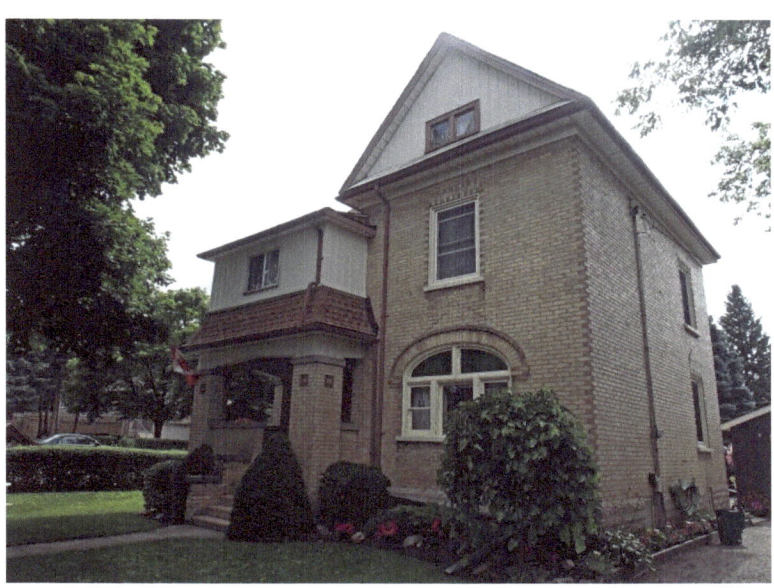

5 Queen Street – Romanesque style window arch
on lower window

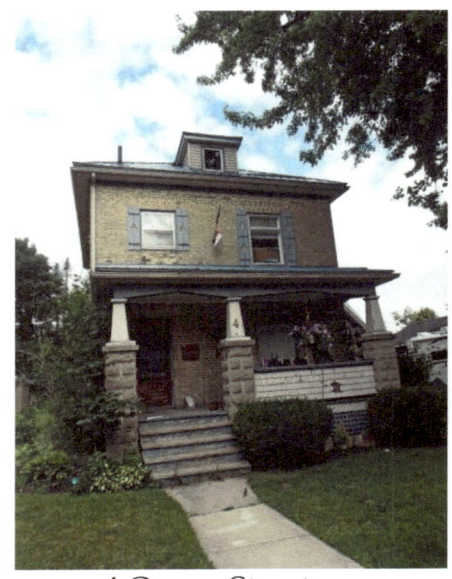

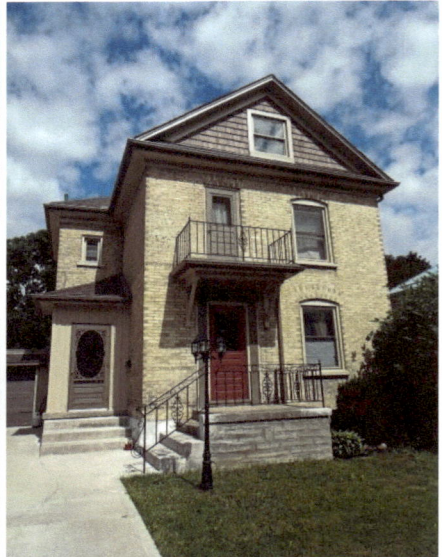

4 Queen Street   6 Queen Street
Italianate, dormer in attic

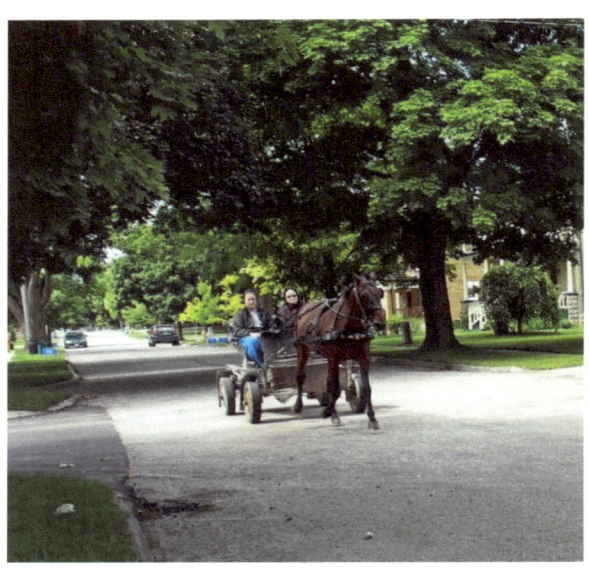

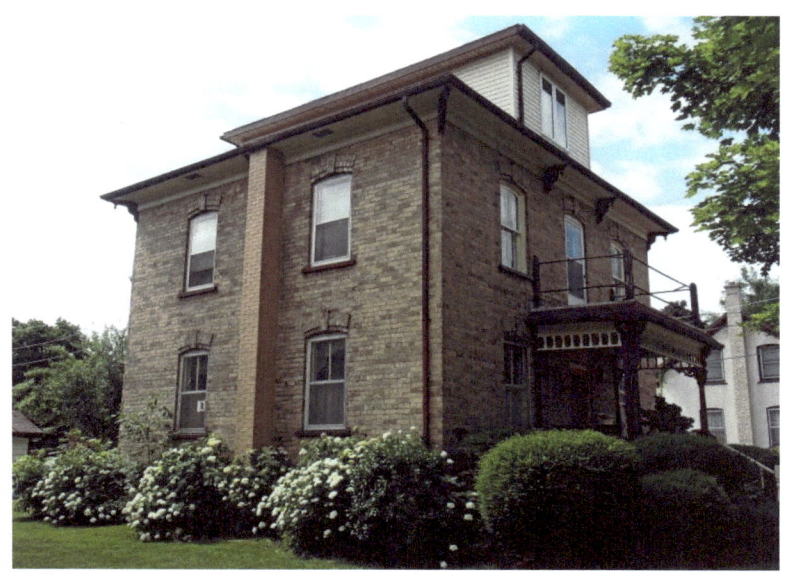

31 Memorial Avenue – Italianate – dormer in attic

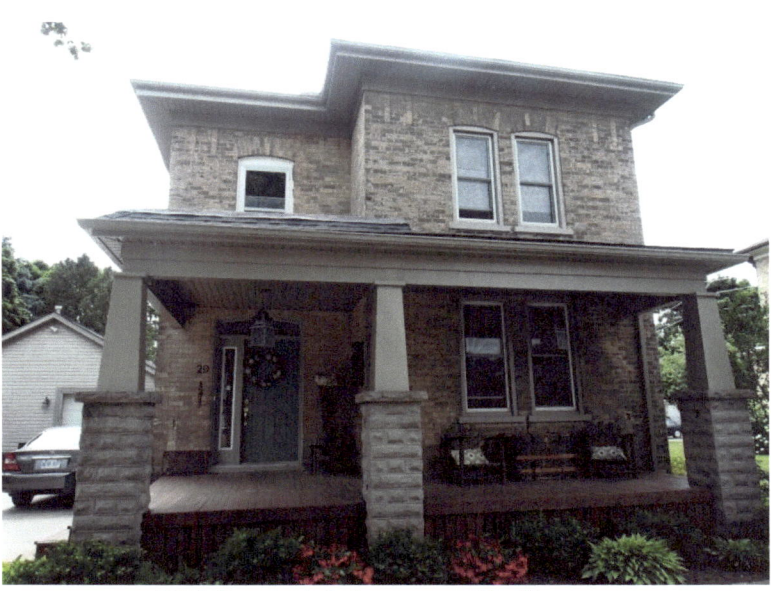

29 Memorial Avenue - Italianate

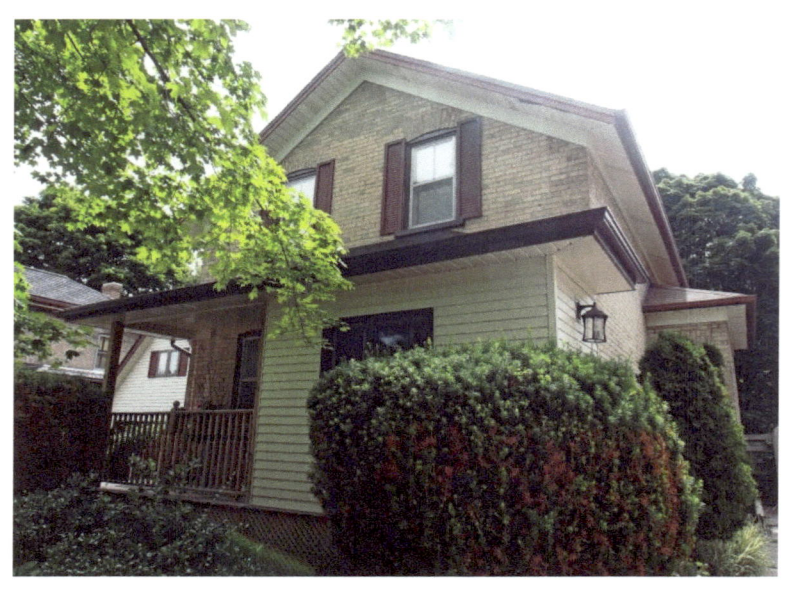

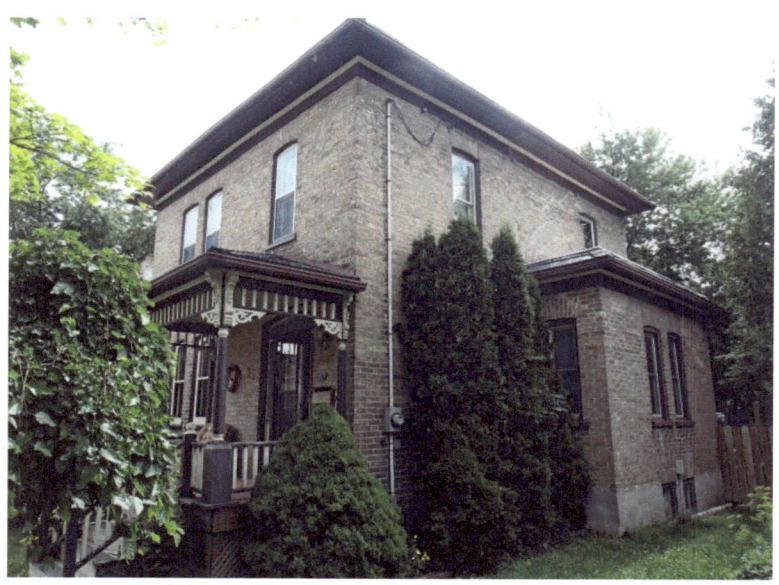

25 Memorial Avenue - Italianate

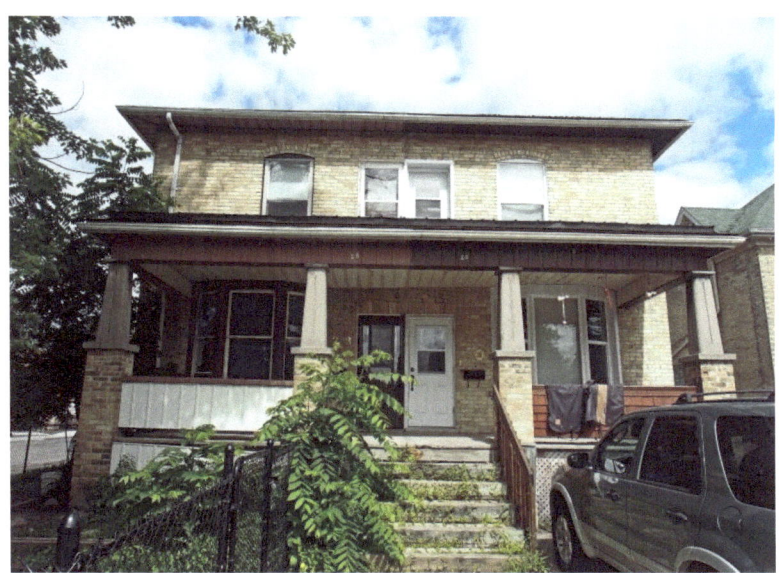

26-28 Memorial Avenue - Italianate

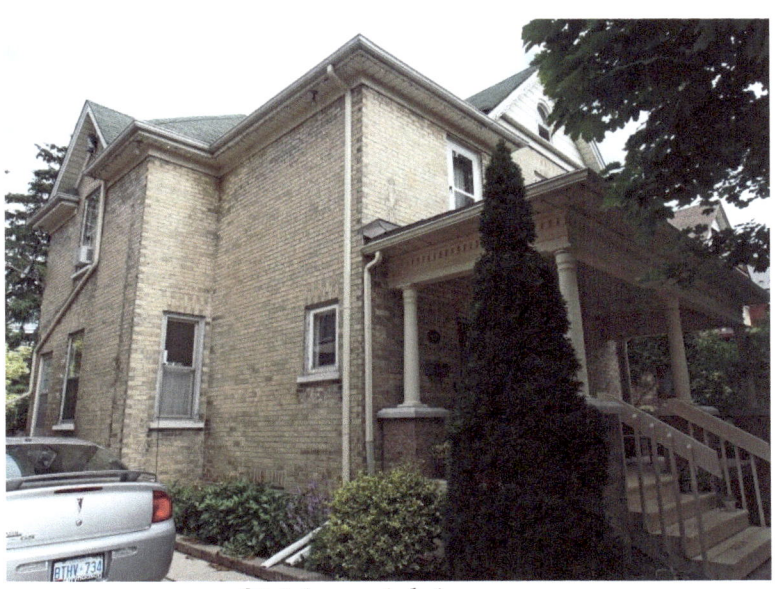

24 Memorial Avenue

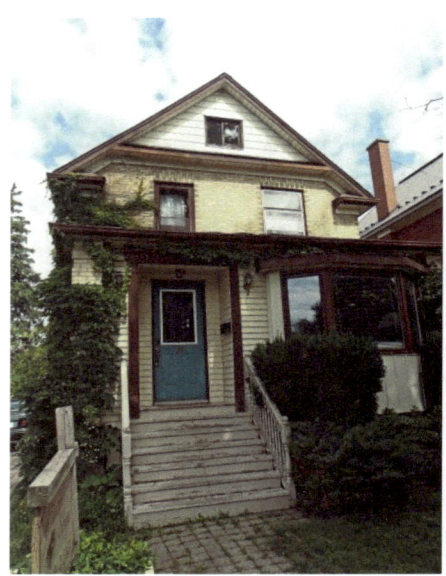

22 Memorial Avenue
Edwardian

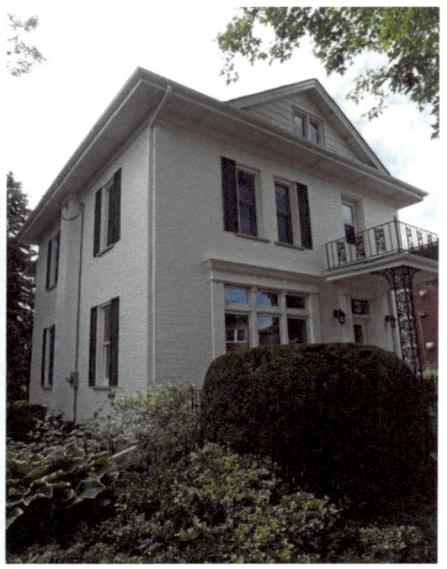

37 Memorial Avenue

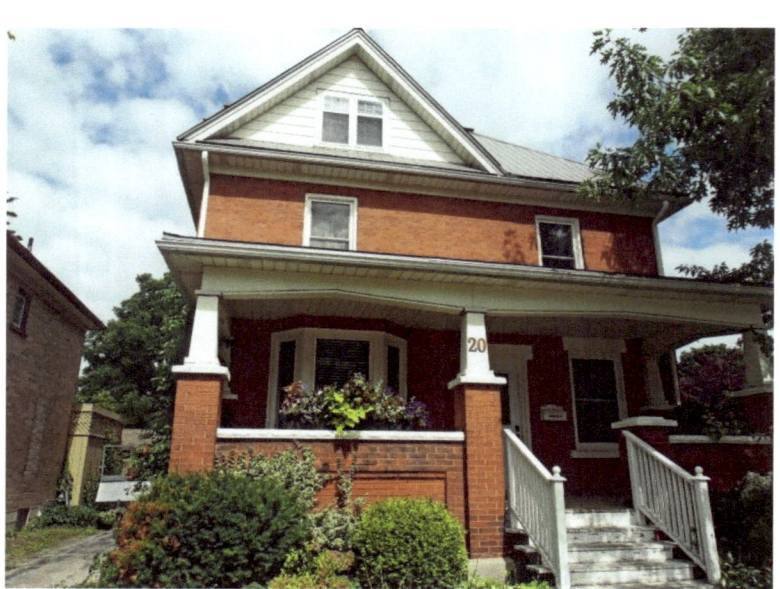

20 Memorial Avenue

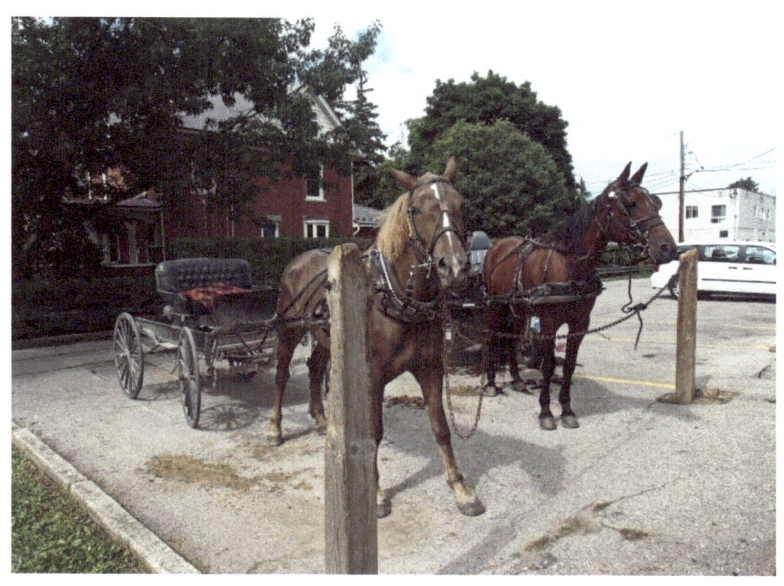

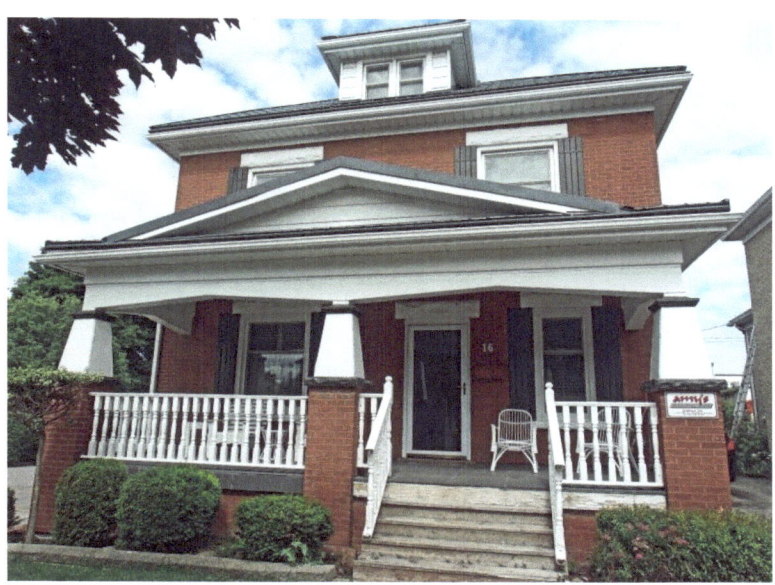

16 Memorial Avenue – Italianate, dormer,
pediment above verandah

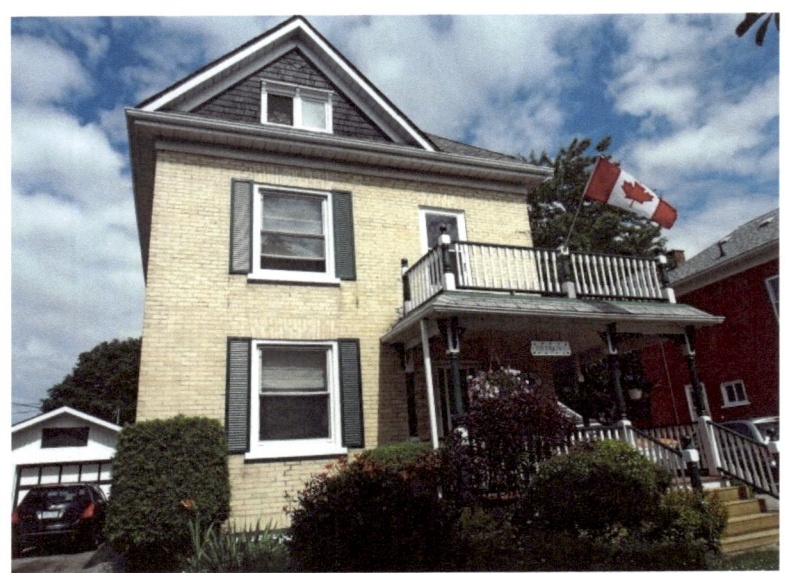

14 Memorial Avenue

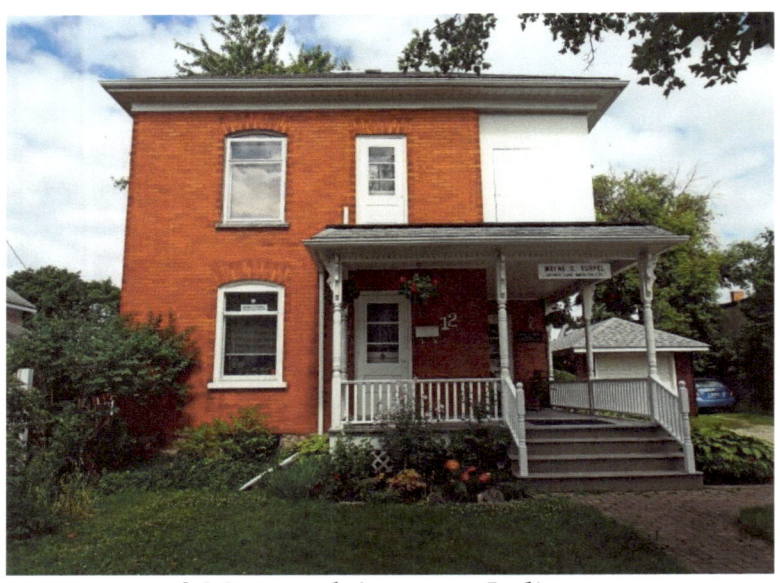

12 Memorial Avenue - Italianate

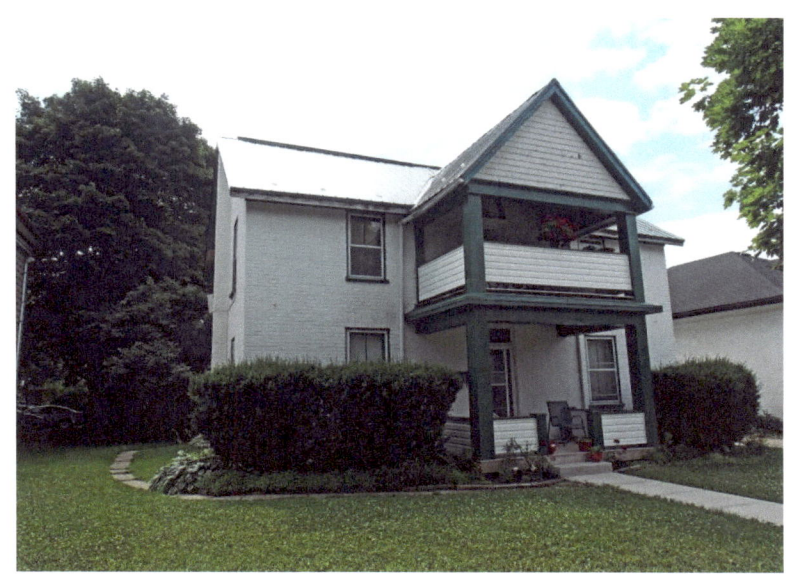

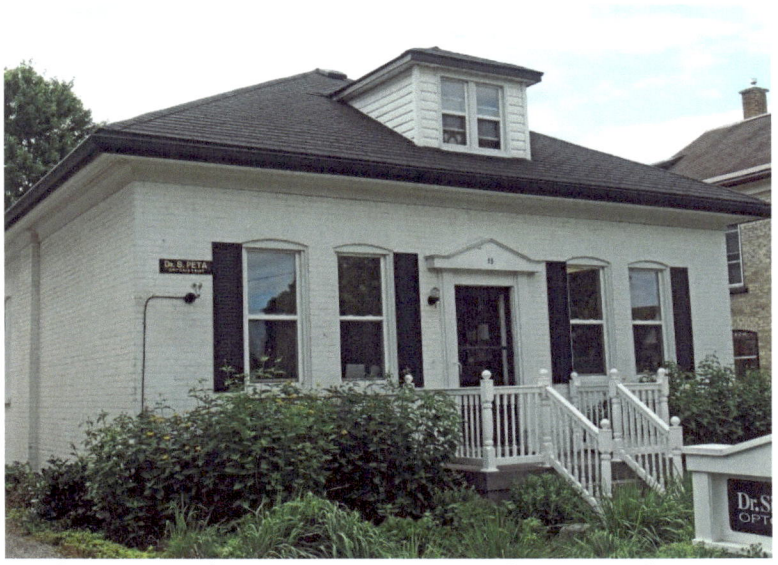

13 Memorial Avenue – Regency Cottage - dormer

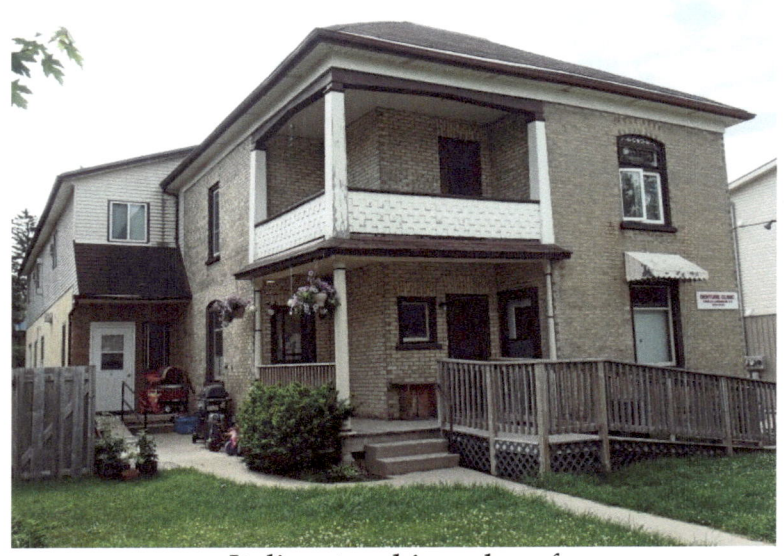

Italianate – hipped roof

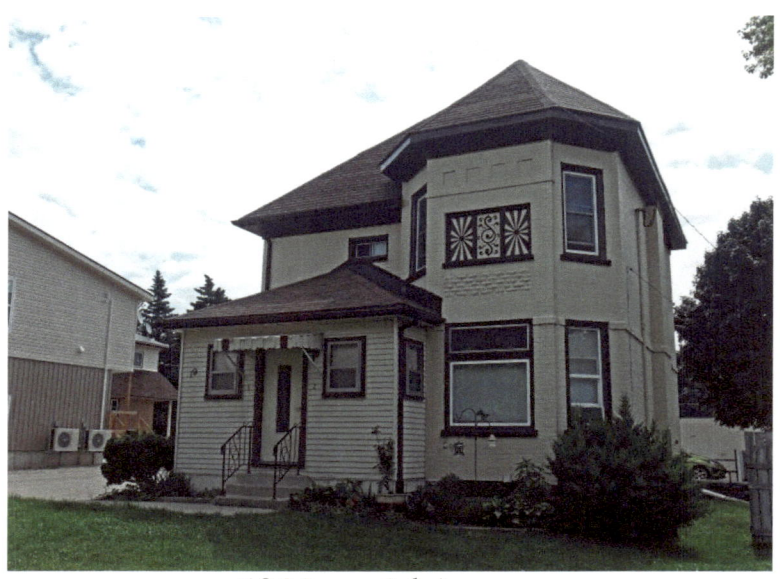

19 Memorial Avenue

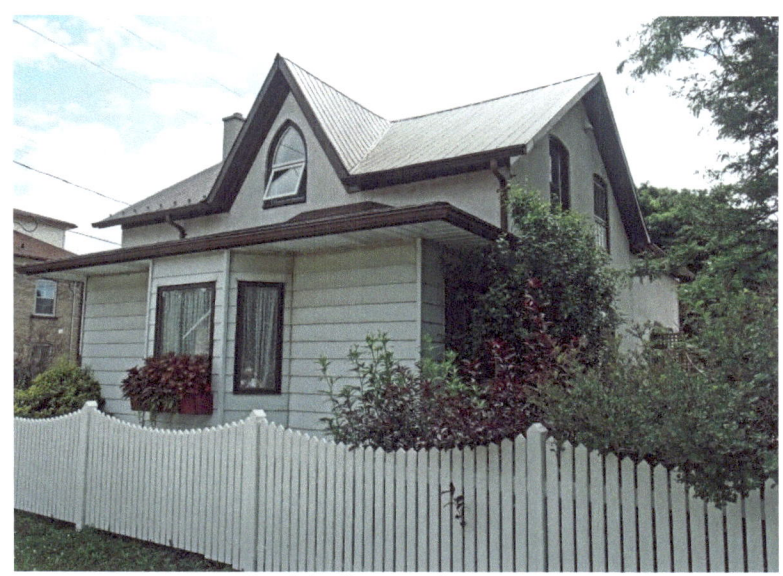

Gothic Revival cottage

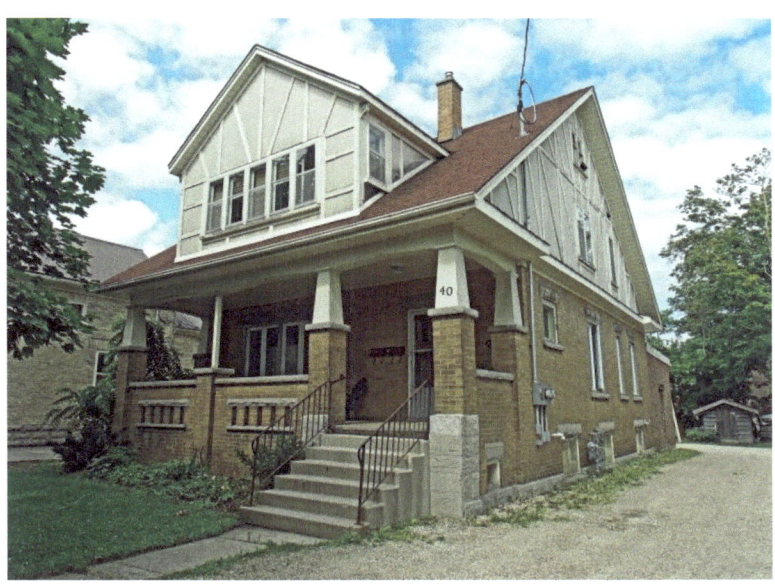

40 Memorial Avenue – Tudor style

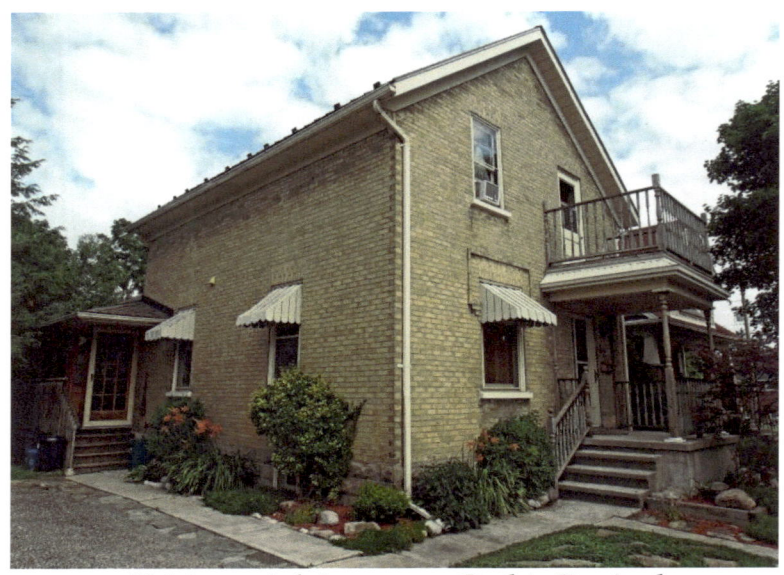

42 Memorial Avenue – Gothic Revival

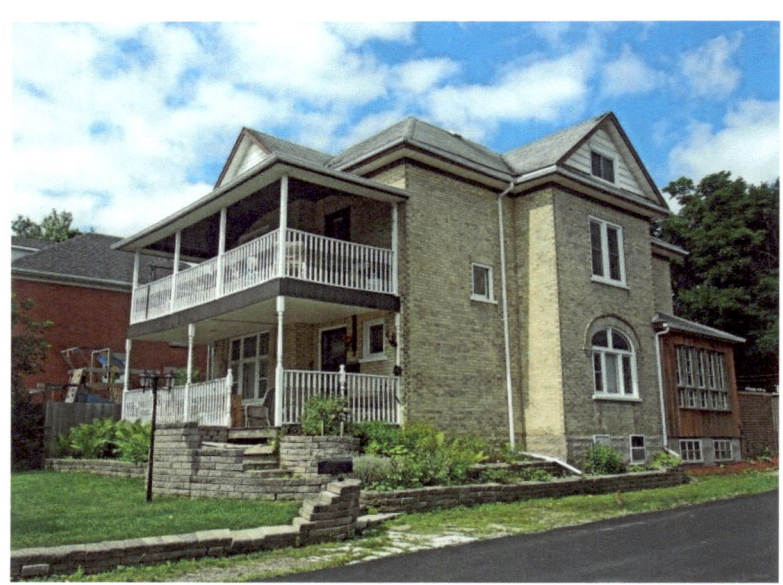

46 Memorial Avenue – Romanesque style window arch on lower side window, balcony on second floor

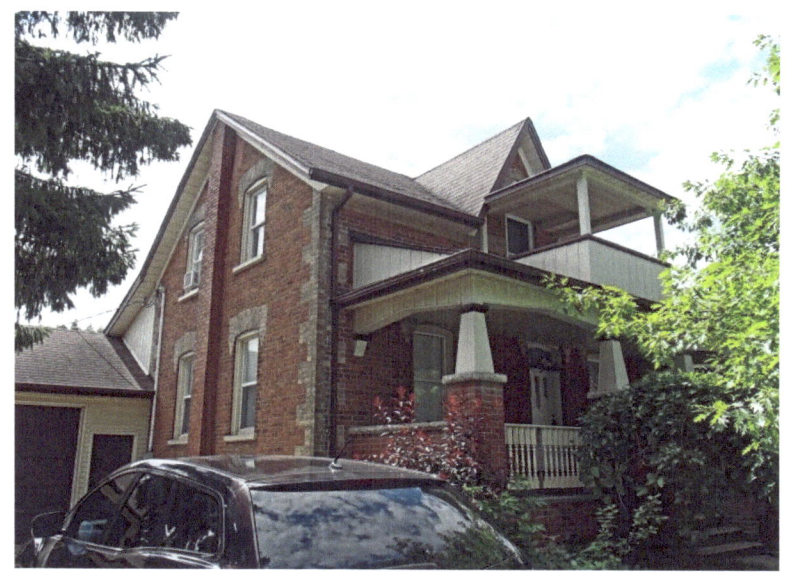

Gothic Revival – corner quoins, balcony on second floor

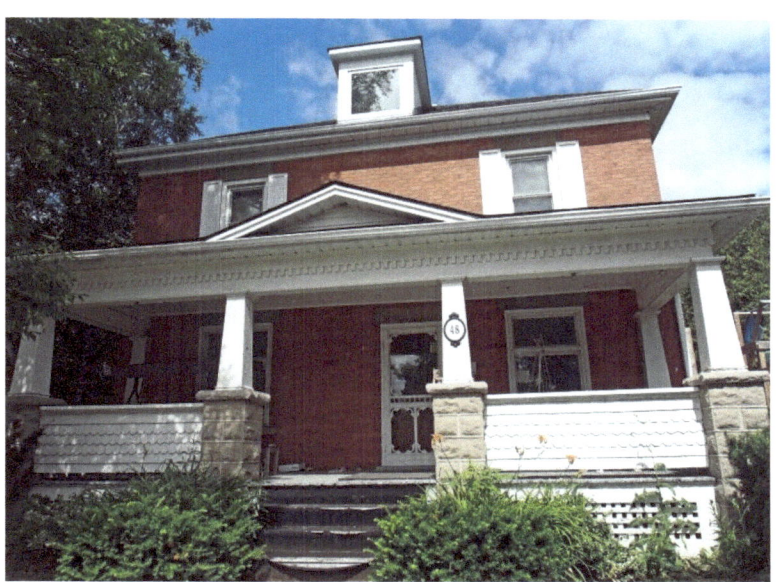

48 Memorial Avenue – Italianate, dormer in attic

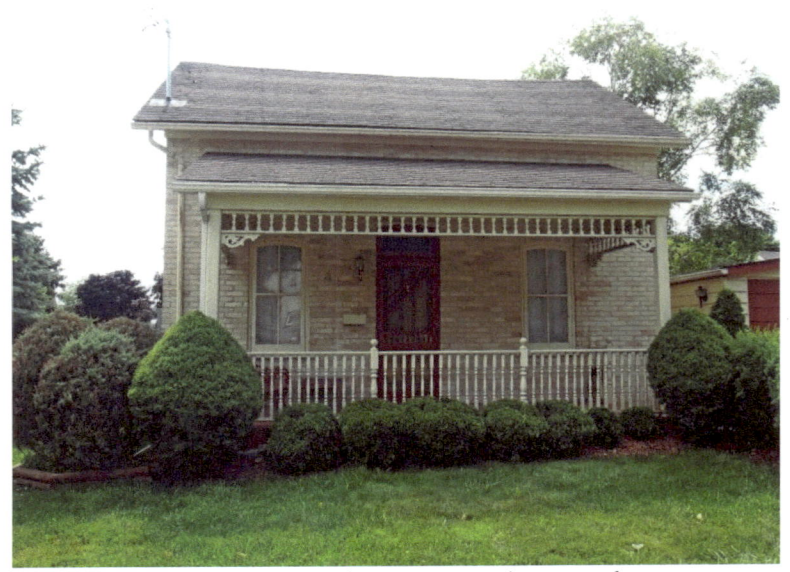

45 Memorial Avenue – hip roof

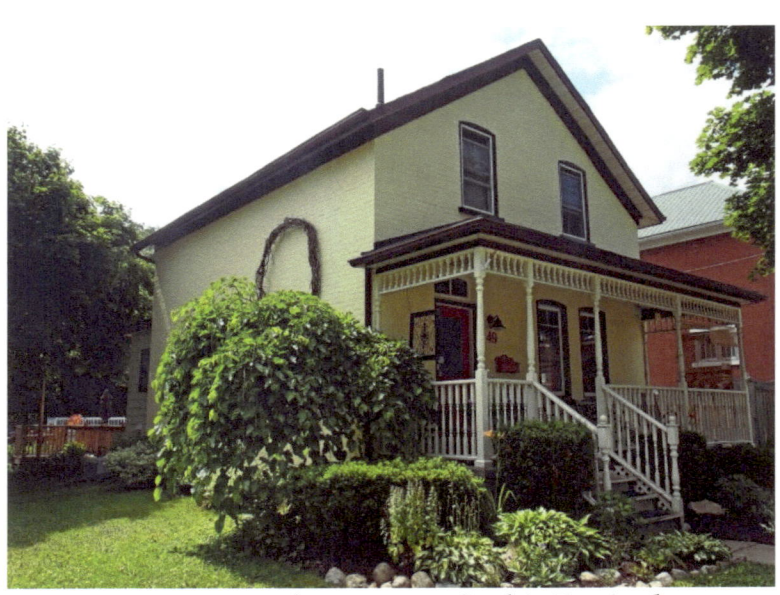

49 Memorial Avenue – Gothic Revival

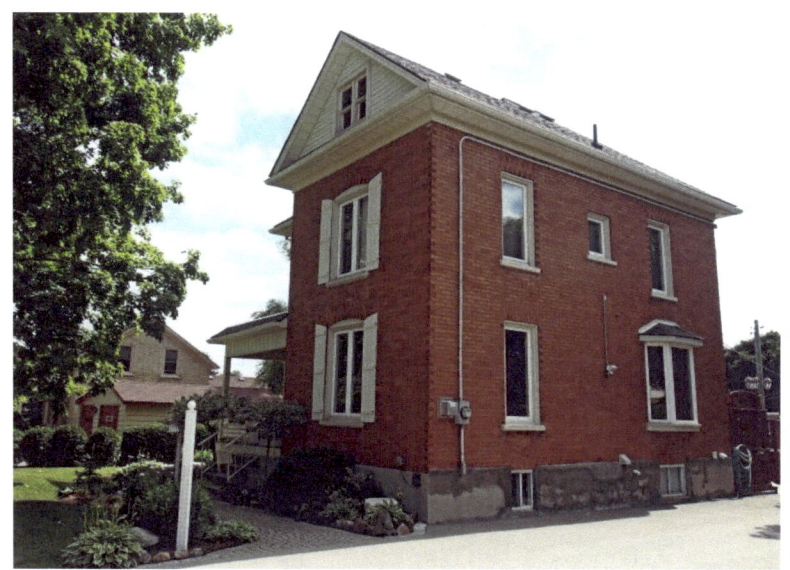

Edwardian

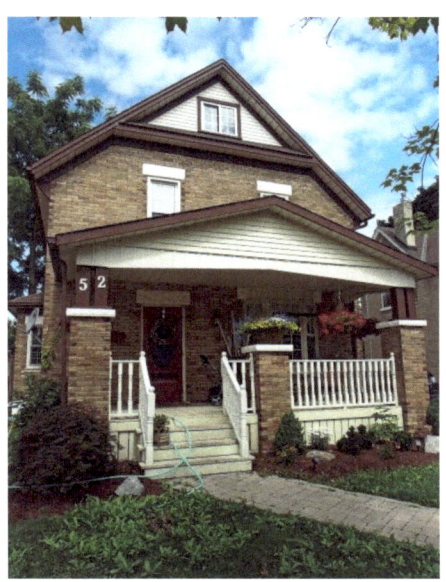

52 Memorial Avenue - Edwardian

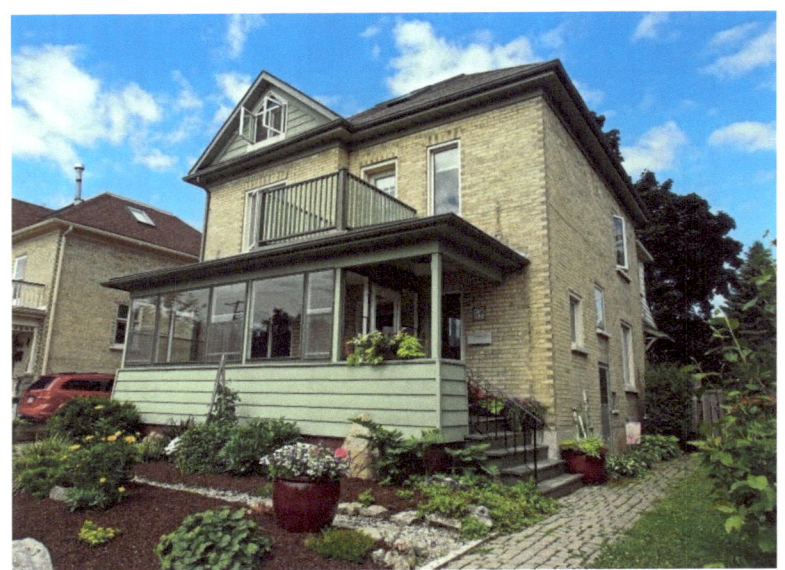

56 Memorial Avenue – Italianate – hipped roof, dormer

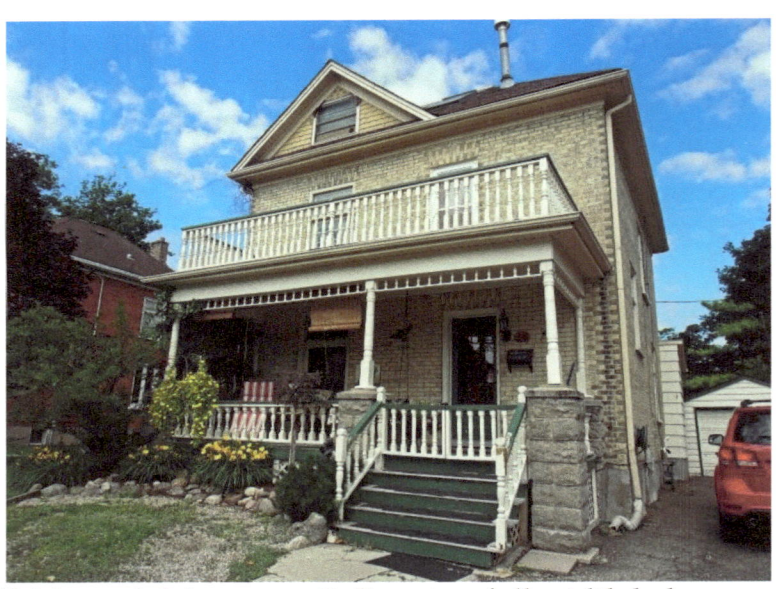

58 Memorial Avenue – Italianate – full width balcony on second floor, dormer

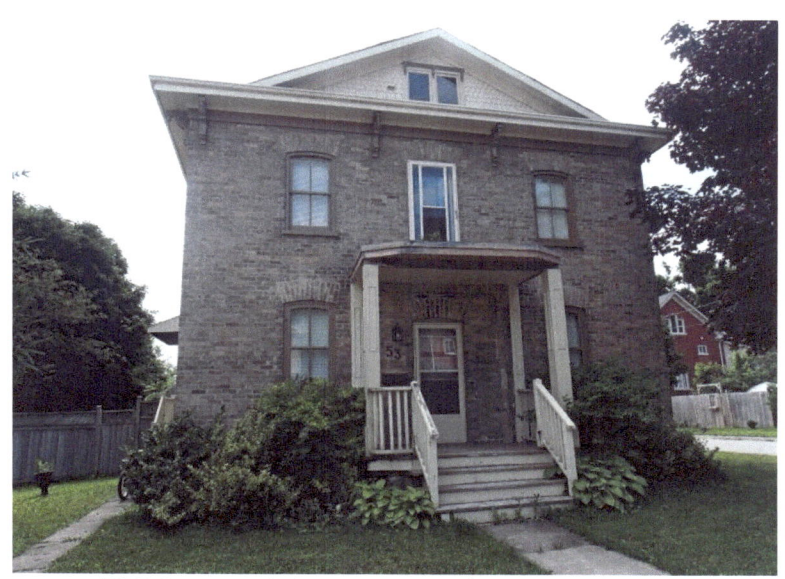

53 Memorial Avenue – Italianate - dormer

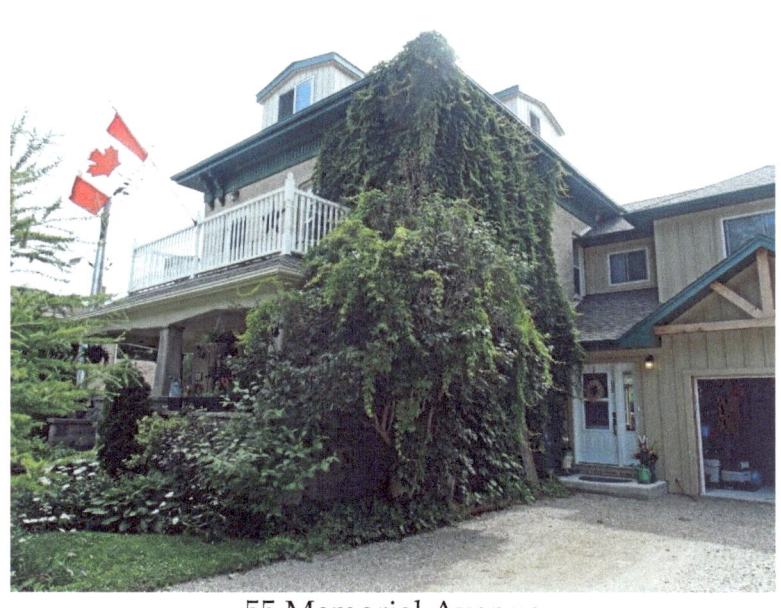

55 Memorial Avenue

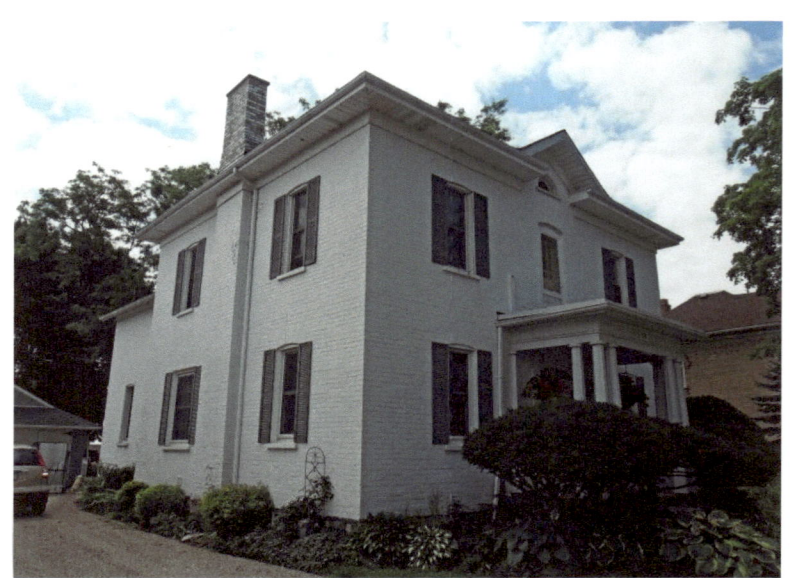

57 Memorial Avenue – Italianate

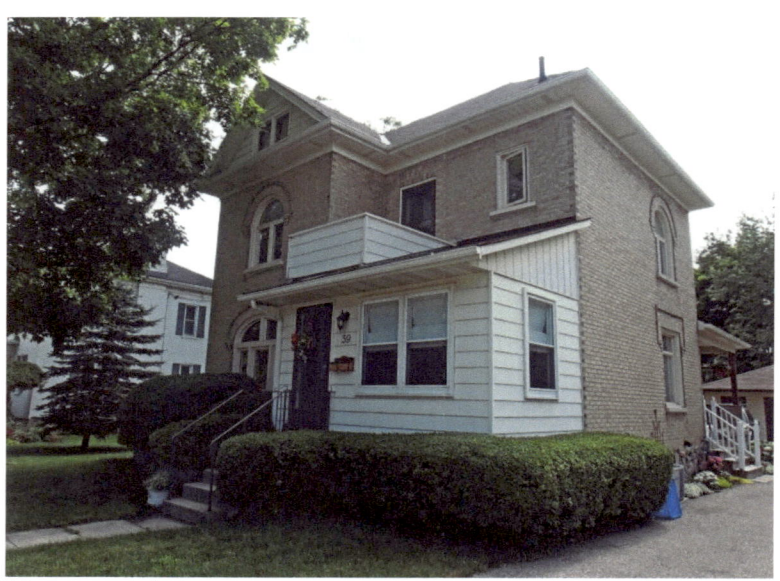

59 Memorial Avenue – Romanesque style window arches

Architectural Terms

Brackets: a decorative or weight-bearing structural element which forms a right angle with one side against a wall and the other under a projecting surface such as an eave or roof. Example: Downtown, Arthur Street South	
Capital: The uppermost finish or decoration on a column. Example: Carnegie Free Library	
Cornice: originally the wooden overhang of the roof. With the use of stone, brick, iron and steel, the cornice is any projecting shelf at the top of a ceiling or roof. They can be very decorative. Example: 57 Memorial Avenue	
Cornice Return: decorative element on the end of a gable. Example: 21 Queen Street	
Dormer: (French for "sleep") a gable end window that pierces through the plane of a sloping roof surface to create usable space in the top floor or attic of a building by adding headroom. Example: 13 Memorial Avenue	

Fretwork: interlaced decorative design resembling a bracket Example: 12 Park Avenue	
Gable: the triangular portion of a wall between the edges of a sloping roof. Example: 23 South Street	
Hipped Roof: a roof where all sides slope downwards to the walls with no gables. Example: 70 Arthur Street South	
Keystones and Voussoirs: a voussoir is a wedge-shaped element used in building an arch. A keystone is the central stone that locks all the stones into position, allowing the arch to bear weight. A keystone is often enlarged and embellished. Example: Arthur Street South	
Lancet Window: a tall, narrow window with a pointed arch at its top. Example: St. James Evangelical Lutheran Church	

Pediment: a triangular section above the horizontal structure (entablature), typically supported by columns. The inside of the triangle is called the tympanum. Example:	
Quoin: masonry blocks at the corner of a wall, often a decorative feature, usually larger or of a different colour than the rest of the wall. Example: Memorial Avenue	
Vergeboard and Finial: also called bargeboards – hang from the projecting end of a roof and are often elaborately carved and ornamented. **Finial:** ornament added to the top of a gable, pinnacle, canopy or spire – a Gothic element. Example: 80 Arthur Street South	

Edwardian, 1900-1930 – This style bridges the ornate and elaborate styles of the Victorian era and the simplified styles of the 20th century. Balanced facades, simple roof lines, dormer windows, large front porches, and smooth brick surfaces are its characteristics. Example: 34 Queen Street	
Gothic Revival, 1830-1890 – These decorative buildings have sharply-pitched gables with highly detailed vergeboards, pointed-arch window openings, and dichromatic brickwork. It is a common style in Ontario. Example: 6 South Street	
Italianate, 1850-1900 – It has wide-bracketed eaves, belvederes, wrap-around verandahs. Example: 62 Arthur Street South	
Queen Anne, 1885-1900 – This style is distinguished by an irregular outline featuring a combination of an offset tower, broad gables, projecting two-storey bays, verandahs, multi-sloped roofs, and tall, decorative chimneys. A mixture of brick and wood is common. Windows often have one large single-paned bottom sash and small panes in the upper sash.	

Romanesque Revival, 1880-1910 – This style hearkens back to medieval architecture of the 11th and 12th centuries with a heavy appearance, blocky towers and rounded arches. Example: Queen Street	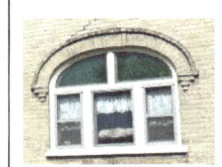
Tudor Revival – exposed timbers with stucco infill, multi-paned windows. Example: 20 South Street	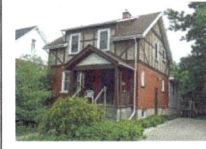

www.ingramcontent.com/pod-product-compliance
Lightning Source LLC
Chambersburg PA
CBHW040847180526
45159CB00001B/342